Dear Parents

Dear Parents

A **FIELD GUIDE** for
COLLEGE PREPARATION

Jon McGee

Foreword by Chris Farrell

JOHNS HOPKINS UNIVERSITY PRESS · BALTIMORE

© 2018 Johns Hopkins University Press
All rights reserved. Published 2018
Printed in the United States of America on acid-free paper
9 8 7 6 5 4 3 2 1

Johns Hopkins University Press
2715 North Charles Street
Baltimore, Maryland 21218-4363
www.press.jhu.edu

Library of Congress Cataloging-in-Publication Data

Names: McGee, Jon, 1962– author.
Title: Dear parents : a field guide for college preparation / Jon McGee ; foreword by
    Chris Farrell.
Description: Baltimore : Johns Hopkins University Press, 2018. | Includes index.
Identifiers: LCCN 2018007459 | ISBN 9781421426839 (pbk : alk. paper) | ISBN
    1421426838 (pbk : alk. paper) | ISBN 9781421426846 (electronic) | ISBN 1421426846
    (electronic)
Subjects: LCSH: College student orientation—United States. | Education, Higher—
    Parent participation—United States. | BISAC: EDUCATION / Higher.
Classification: LCC LB2343.32.M423 2018 | DDC 378.1/98—dc23
LC record available at https://lccn.loc.gov/2018007459

A catalog record for this book is available from the British Library.

*Special discounts are available for bulk purchases of this book. For more information,
please contact Special Sales at 410-516-6936 or specialsales@press.jhu.edu.*

Johns Hopkins University Press uses environmentally friendly book materials, including
recycled text paper that is composed of at least 30 percent post-consumer waste, when-
ever possible.

For Andrew, Nick, Ben, and Kate
Oh, the places you'll go!

Contents

Foreword

Heading off to college is an act of optimism for both parents and their young adult. Whether it's community college, technical school, private liberal arts campus, or downtown public university, young adults take a major step toward finding their place in the world and carving their own path when they enter college. We may live in a grumpy era, but if you spend time on a college campus visiting with students, you can't help but believe the world will become a better place.

All right, time to take out your No. 2 pencils.

When it comes to postsecondary education:
   a. Graduates are paid more than their high school degree–only peers
   b. Graduates have lower rates of unemployment than less educated workers
   c. Both of the above

Students borrow more to pay for college because:
   a. College costs have risen faster than the consumer price index
   b. Family incomes have stagnated
   c. Both of the above

The purpose of financial aid is:
   a. To close the gap between what families can afford to pay and the price of college
   b. To confuse parents with unrealistic estimates of ability to pay
   c. Both of the above

Go to the head of the class if you answered "c" to all three questions.

Little wonder college is controversial. A cottage industry of critics has gained an audience claiming postsecondary credentials aren't worth the time and cost. An easy way to spark a fierce discussion at a neighborhood barbeque or during a lunch break at work is to ask why college costs so much. You can fan the flames of discussion by bringing up the convoluted financial aid system and its arcane formulas. It's a reasonable bet if Mark Twain were alive today he'd modify his famous quip about the certainty of "death and taxes" to include "college tuition goes up every year."

That said, parents know from experience that college graduates have lower rates of unemployment and higher wages than their less-educated peers. Postsecondary education is a necessary but not sufficient condition (to paraphrase the philosophers) for young adults to have an opportunity to land the kinds of jobs and careers that pay well and offer prospects for creativity and development. College is an incendiary topic because the stakes are so high.

Put it this way: college is expensive, but not earning postsecondary credentials is even more costly measured over a lifetime. This calculation comes before taking into account intangible benefits from higher education. "I think students come out of college as better citizens, as more thoughtful members of their communities, maybe with different cultural tastes and cultural tendencies than they would have otherwise," said Michael McPherson, the former president of Macalester College, in an interview years ago. "For many people, it's the most valuable investment they are going to make."

McPherson is spot on.

So is Jon McGee. If you've picked up this book, my guess is you don't need convincing that there is a lifelong return from a college education. You want to understand the process better and you'd like to help your teen smartly navigate their choices. You picked wisely if that's the case. The reality is there are many good higher education options for young people, and with some planning there is no reason to saddle young adults (or parents) with steep debt burdens. Jon is a wonderful guide, shedding light on the mysterious process of applying to college while bringing much insight to the inevitable trade-offs.

However, like me, you may find the real value lies in reading the intangibles expressed by parents, including Jon, looking back on their experience with their students. A major takeaway of the letters in this book is the common desire parents have for their children to be engaged and curious throughout their lives, to find a path toward both meaning and money when they launch their own lives and careers. As parents, we've been around long enough to realize how much curiosity and discovery will hold them in good stead throughout the ups and downs they'll confront long after graduation. Your student will have many careers, many jobs, and many enthusiasms.

Vice President Joe Biden captured the essence of the letters Jon gathered in this book in a 2015 commencement speech at Yale University, paraphrasing an expression of his father. "It's a lucky man or woman who gets up in the morning, puts both feet on the floor, knows what they're about to do, and thinks it still matters," Biden said. That's what we want for our children.

The particulars of how to best nourish that sense of curiosity and the search for meaning take many paths during the college years. You'll read about parents embracing gap years, community and technical college, full-time job and part-time schooling, and the classic experience of the full-time student on campus. It's fascinating to read how children growing up in the same household can be so different. A choice that works wonders for one teen may not be the right decision for another child.

Sending a child to college elicits many emotions. Did you know it's possible to be extremely happy and deeply sad at the same time? That's how I felt when we dropped off each of our two children at college and when we watched them graduate four years later. They learned so much. They made lifelong friends. I'm sure they had adventures I still don't know about (thank you). They're carving out their own paths with careers and relationships. College was an integral part of their journey, but college is also one step—to be sure a big one—in a lifetime of continuous learning.

Happily, they've grown up to become young adults that fulfill every parent's wish: they turned out better than their parents. Best of all, they still call and visit!

Chris Farrell
Marketplace

Prologue

IN THE BEGINNING

Dear Parents,

I came of age during the late 1960s and 1970s, likely the last generation of "free-range children," living a good portion of my early years independent of the watchful, hovering eyes of parents. Born near the tail end of the baby-boom generation, my young life was defined by kids. Lots of kids. The street where I grew up teemed with children. The classrooms in our schools were jammed with students. We roamed in packs, from ballparks to swimming lessons to schools and to malls. Like any other kid, I spent no time thinking about what it meant to be a parent. Our parents were just parents. Born to understand what we needed and wanted. What else was there to know? As kids, we more or less lived for the moment—the next game, the next class, or the next activity. The future seemed a distant prospect and, in any case, that was something our parents were supposed to worry about, not us. The sweet naiveté of youth.

Fast-forward: adulthood. As my wife and I walked out of the hospital holding our first born on a cold November day in Saint Paul, Minnesota, in 1996, one question looped through the soundtrack of my mind: Where is his owner's manual? Any confidence we may have had after weeks of birthing classes vanished with the reality that parenthood was no longer an illusion or a fantasy. It was real. Our son was ours to feed, clothe, care for, and raise. He did not come to us with an owner's manual, though he immediately expressed both his needs and his demands.

My wife and I had every reason for confidence. We had waited to have children and were both in our early thirties. We each had good

1

careers—my wife's as an elementary school teacher, which at least to me seemed to confer some deep understanding of how children worked. We both grew up in large, supportive families. Many of our friends already had children and freely offered us advice and tips. Still, the moment the door opened to the waiting world, none of that seemed to matter. Now what? (For the record, I failed my first test of parenthood. After driving home from the hospital on icy roads, I discovered that I had not securely or safely fastened the car seat. I still have nightmares about car seats.)

So began our journey of parenthood, a trek defined by trial and error, ecstasy and sometimes agony, and framed by an abiding love of our children. Thousands of websites, books, and magazines offer a range of practical, philosophic, and often humorous insights about what it means to parent. But there is no precise definition of parent or parenting. It is the ultimate on-the-job experience. We learn as we go. Three more children later, my wife and I have learned much about ourselves and about life. But we still don't have an owner's manual.

College. The word conjures a variety of emotions, from anxiety and fear to pride and admiration. For new parents, it typically seems an unimaginably distant prospect. Eighteen years may as well be a century in the sleep-deprived, car seat days. During those early years, fuzzy pajamas demand more attention than fuzzy futures. For parents of high school–age children, college appears as a timer, ticking down to a zero hour. "Is college the right choice? What kind of college is best? What can we afford? Will my child be ready?" For parents dropping their daughter or son off at college, college often evokes simultaneous feelings of joy and sadness. It signals a significant step toward independence and adulthood, but also a significant family change. "Has my child made the right choice? Will my son or daughter be happy? What will happen to them?" In the hullabaloo of the moment, new college students often forget that it is a time of transition not just for them but for their parents and families, too.

At its most antiseptic, college is often described and considered through a series of numbers: rankings in guidebooks, acceptance rates, academic profiles, student-to-faculty ratios, the percentage of students who live on or off campus or who study abroad, retention and graduation rates, percentage of recent graduates who are employed, and the earnings of alumni, among many others. Each of those numbers communicates something important that can be useful to parents and prospective students as they navigate the world of college choice. But each puts us at risk of depersonalizing what ultimately is an exceptionally personal experience: the act of choosing a college, the act of learning and developing as a person, and the act of selecting a life path that is exciting and fulfilling. Guidebook summaries and handy numeric mnemonics describing how much and how many almost never capture the intensity of emotion that underlies both the college choice and the college experience.

I have spent much of my career studying the influence of economic and demographic trends in college enrollment and how students make their college choice, the last seventeen years as head of planning at the College of Saint Benedict and Saint John's University in Minnesota. It is fascinating work—at least to me—that helps us to better understand our students. But I also am a parent of four children who now span the ages of 13 to 21. Unimaginable as we headed home from the hospital in November 1996, in the fall of 2015 our oldest headed off to college, the beginning of a postsecondary parade that will not end for our family until 2028.

During my oldest son's senior year of high school, I nearly sent my wife over the edge when I casually announced that, to finish financing our four children's elementary, secondary, and collegiate education, we could face costs that totaled more than $1 million over the next fifteen years—a gulp-worthy sum by any definition. As we went through our first son's college search and selection process, I learned and experienced what I thought I already knew (but didn't really): although it may be interesting and important to view college through my professional lens of numeracy and social science, most people don't make decisions that way. Both the process and the choice are deeply emotional, forcing an examination of both mind and heart. These are our children, after all, the people we have taught and cajoled and nurtured and loved for eighteen years. Though I have spent decades working in higher education, my wife and I experienced the emotions all parents experience as they wind through their college search—the same hopes, fears, and doubts. We learned through experience that divining rods pointing to an obvious or singular choice did not exist. Nor was there an easy-to-follow, start-to-finish manual to help guide our thinking for the many steps along the way.

Parents play an integral role in the college search process, and not just at the point of application, selection, or paying the bill. It starts as soon as our children arrive. The educational, financial, and parenting choices we make when our kids are young influence who our daughters and sons are, who they will become, and the postsecondary choices they (and we) will later have. Each fall after the new class arrives at the College of Saint Benedict and Saint John's University, I point out to our faculty and staff that none of our students comes to us as a blank slate. Each new student arrives not only with an easy-to-capture-and-describe academic and socioeconomic profile, but also with a set of social, cultural, and personal values and characteristics and a set of lived experiences that shape who they are and to what they aspire—much of that influenced by their parents and their family experiences.

At the same time, though, college often is among the first—and biggest—"adult" or life-path decisions our children make. It's an important one, a choice that will form and influence their professional and personal lives in the decades to follow. The line between what's yours, mine, and ours sometimes blurs. Preparing for college and selecting a college requires a kind of trust walk for parents and students alike. We try to provide our children with enough guidance at each step along the way to position them to make a decision they ultimately must own and will experience.

At a professional presentation I made to parents of high school juniors a couple of years ago, a mom raised her hand and asked, with no small amount of fear in her voice, "What happens if my daughter makes a bad choice?" Though she did not indicate what constituted a "bad choice," her tone suggested that she was seeking help to identify "the one best" college for her daughter. It was a fair question, frequently asked by parents, though not one easily answered. The value of college lies in the whole of its experience—from start to finish. Though difficult to understand at times, if for no other reason than the cost involved, no college experience comes with a guarantee, in part because students themselves shape and define their experience, independent of the institution they choose. More simply put, students are the primary input to their own college output and outcome: their own level of aspiration, preparation, perspiration, and commitment makes an extraordinary difference in the ways they experience college and the outcomes they will derive from it.

So, how to answer this mom? I chose a response I am certain she was not looking for or expecting, but one that captured what I think parents most need to know: the only bad choice is an unconsidered choice. College features, images, and "brands" are seductive. That is by design. But the images too often are limited to the sensory and struggle to get to the heart of the matter. Before our kids make their college choice or even begin the search process, they need to understand first what makes them tick. "Who am I? What do I expect? What do I value most? What do I need?" Parents play a significant role in guiding them to that self-understanding.

I have presented this book through the viewpoint of letters to parents, most of them written by parents of college-age or precollege-age children. The letter writers work at or with colleges, universities, and secondary schools across the country, public and private, some highly selective, others not. Each writer is a leader in some way at his or her school or organization. I asked them to offer their best advice to themselves: How did they prepare themselves and their children for college? What did they learn from their own experiences? The letters are personal because the process a family goes through to select a college and enroll in college is deeply personal, not antiseptic or algorithmic. I have woven in research about college preparation and choice, as well as personal and professional stories of my own throughout, learned and experienced over many years. Like all of my letter-writing colleagues, I am still learning. (And I have three children yet to send off to college.)

I have organized the book around broad chapters that mostly define the stages of childhood (and parenthood) leading up to college as well as the process of searching for and selecting a college. I begin introducing the vast landscape of higher education and the nearly overwhelming number of choices available to students, addressing questions about what college is, its value, and early learning preparation and planning when children are young. What follows is mostly chronological, a walk through the various stages of preparation for college as our children age. Early chapters delve into habits of success in school and how parents can guide their children through their school years. The middle chapters discuss a sometimes overlooked but key piece of the admission process, fit, as well as the most anxiety-inducing issue for most families, how to prepare for and finance a college education for their children. The final chapters attempt to demystify the college selection process and help parents guide their children on matters of applying to and choosing a college. I conclude with insights about sending children off to college and the appropriate roles for parents as their children experience these important years of their lives.

This work is not a guidebook about how to select or "get into" a specific college or university. Nor is it an investment guide or a step-by-step tool describing how to complete a college application. In other words, it is not an owner's manual. Rather, I offer it to you parents as a set of insights, guidance, and, hopefully, wisdom—a field guide of sorts—about college, college preparation, and college choice at the various stages of your children's lives. My aim is not to prescribe but to empower, and in the process perhaps reduce some of the anxiety and stress that have come to define the college search process.

Parenting is a complex business and hard work. Hopefully, parents talking to parents can ease the burden a bit and help to light the path. Enjoy these years. As all parents of college students come to realize, they pass much too quickly.

All the best,

Jon McGee
Cold Spring, Minnesota

ONE

Discover College

We don't see things as they are, we see them as we are.
—**Anaïs Nin**

 From Pam Horne, Vice Provost for Enrollment Management (Retired), Purdue University, Indiana

Dear Parents,

I spent my entire forty-three-year career in higher education. Over that time, I worked with thousands of families, lived through my two daughters' transitions from high school to college, and learned many important lessons.

Long ago, when our children were very young, my husband and I agreed that our job as parents was to raise competent and responsible adults. Keeping that goal in mind provided us a solid framework for our children's transition from high school to college, an important step in their development as young adults. Along the way, we learned that the path is different for different children and not always straight.

My older daughter could have been the poster child for early choice and clarity, discovering her dream college on vacation when she was just 14 years old. She stuck to that dream throughout her high school years and applied early. Happily, she was admitted and thrived, taking advantage of everything the college had to offer both on campus and off. Simple. We had an entirely different experience with our younger daughter. Unlike her sister, she was indecisive. She ultimately considered two outstanding institutions but did not settle on her decision until the very end of the admission process. Although she had a good experience, I cannot honestly say she flourished in college or fully experienced her institution. Two children, two experiences.

In spite of the differences in their experiences, both of our children turned out just fine—each building a successful career and living a good adult life. The lesson was clear: many paths, and often detours, can lead to success. Your daughter or son might want to experience a different part of the country, stay close to home, commute, or even take a gap year. They may enroll at one school and transfer to another. More than half of all students will change majors at least once. Our children will not always get what they (or we) want, and they may not follow the straightest or simplest path, but that's not always a bad thing. Encourage your child to chart their course and own their college search and choice process. Admission is not a grade on parenting.

Ultimately, college is what a student makes of it. I have always believed that, but new research confirms that how one goes to college is more important than where a student enrolls. The Gallup organization has surveyed thousands of college alumni and found that several types of involvements and relationships in college are strongly associated with great careers and thriving personal lives.[1] Institutional characteristics such as rankings, cost, number of students enrolled, or type of institution (private or public) matter little in terms of outcomes. Instead, Gallup found that engagement is key, particularly in sustained long-term projects, student organizations, and internships. Meaningful relationships also are important. Mentors, professors who make learning exciting, and others who care about each student as a person make an extraordinary difference.

What does it all mean for our children? Learning how to communicate is vital. Asking for help when needed is a sign of strength, not weakness. Finding involvement outside of the classroom that complements academic study and meets personal interests is not a distraction but rather a ticket to leadership and community. And finally, networking and developing diverse relationships and a love of alma mater contribute to future success. So parents, teach your children well about problem solving, interpersonal communication, and resilience. They will be grateful you taught them how to make choices, recover from mistakes and setbacks, develop great relationships, pursue their dreams, and manage their lives.

Through the Looking Glass

Each of my parents was the first in their family to go to college, both of them in the 1950s. For them and their families, higher education represented a completely new experience. A generation later, they sent their four children off to college. Though my parents never told us we had to go to college or to a certain kind of college, growing up I only ever imagined myself enrolling at a four-year school much like the ones my parents had attended. College, a path I simply assumed, meant something very particular and very familiar.

Now as my own four children begin to complete high school and prepare for the next stage of their lives, I often find myself retreating to the temptation of my familiar, thinking about college for them in the same way I experienced it myself. On reflection, the lesson is simple. We frequently shape our dreams, preferences, and expectations for our children through the prism of our own experiences. We understand what is and what we think should be through what is most familiar or comfortable or known to us. Thinking that way can open doors in many cases but may close them in others. Our familiarity with what we know, as well as our perceptions or even fears about what we don't know, often frame our choices, not just for ourselves but also for our kids. Unfortunately, when it comes to college, that prism may be too narrow—not reflecting the vast array of choices our children actually have or, worse, being out of sync with their abilities or aspirations.

Over many years, I have learned that almost everyone has some impression of college and the college experience, good, bad, or otherwise. For some, those impressions come from having gone to college. For others, they come from movies or media images (think *Legally Blonde* or *Animal House*). For others still, from sports. When my kids were young, they routinely asked if the schools they watched play in football bowl games or tournament basketball games were "good schools." Experience and image exert a powerful influence on perception.

Before you take your first look at a college admission publication, peruse a college website, or visit a campus with your daughter or son, take a moment to think about your own image of college. What comes to mind? What does "college" mean to you? That's important, because how we think about it as parents—what college is and what we expect from it—shapes how we will influence and guide our children's choices.

As you begin thinking about your child's educational future, I encourage you to take a wide view of the many opportunities available. Don't limit yourself to an exclusive focus on what you think you know best or prejudge what may be less familiar to you or not at all familiar to you. My friend Frank Sachs, longtime college counselor at the Blake Schools in Minneapolis, for years has included this bit of advice in his email salutation: "College is a match to be made, not a prize to be won." I thought about that a lot during my oldest son's college search. It is wise counsel, worth reciting frequently, as we guide our children to their future.

Grace

My niece Grace graduated with honors from high school in Chanhassen, Minnesota, a couple of years ago. She took the requisite college preparatory courses common among kids attending suburban high schools, sprinkling her regular school curriculum with a fistful of Advanced Placement (AP) courses and even college courses at a local community college. She was the kind of student most colleges spend a lot of time trying to recruit and enroll: bright, articulate, hard-working, and confident. Everything about her preparation suggested she would follow a traditional path, choosing a four-year college similar to the ones her parents—and all of her immediate family—had chosen. Only she didn't.

Grace will soon complete a two-year degree program in machine tool technology at Alexandria Technical College in central Minnesota. Upon graduation, she will enter the workforce as a skilled machinist, creating tools and parts that make car engines run, airplanes fly, and industrial equipment hum. She hardly projects the image of a machine tool specialist. She is not quite five feet tall, petite, and female in a profession dominated by men. She is one of only three women at her school enrolled in the machine tool technology program. Her toolbox is nearly as tall as she is. She often works on equipment that requires her to stand on pallets for added reach. But Grace has always had the rare gift of being comfortable in her own skin and resolute about her goals, willing to pursue what many others would politely, and sometimes not so politely, describe as "nontraditional." This is her higher education dream. Her parents, both of whom had traditional four-year undergraduate experiences, have supported her dream throughout.

Grace had a wide variety of college choices and considered mechanical engineering. She chose a program in machine tool technology because she finds joy working with tools and making things. She also views herself as a pathbreaker. In a scholarship essay, she wrote:

> Throughout my life, I have had the privilege to make many things, from hammers to my identity, to my presence as a minority woman in a male-dominated career field. Through all of these projects, I have learned to keep working hard, to never give up on my dreams, and to never let anyone tell me what I can or cannot do. I hope to chart a path for female machinists and to build a career for myself that I can be proud of.

Her choice will almost certainly pay off economically; graduates of her program are in high demand and often command comfortable starting salaries. But that's not really the point. Grace made a choice, with her parents' blessing and support, to pursue a goal that clearly aligned her interests with her aspirations—an outcome most parents dream about (particularly if it also comes with economic independence).

I deeply admire Grace's college choice, her goals, and her courage. She had to endure a summer of questions between high school graduation and heading off to college. Asked in a variety of quizzical ways, the questions generally reflected a singular point of view: "Why would you do *that* instead of getting a four-year degree?" The inquisitors, typically well-educated upper-middle-class adults, could not understand how an honor student would choose a technical college degree program—a choice that lived outside the framework of their understanding and experience of college. Her answers were spot on. "I wanted to do something that I'd never get tired of," she told me. "What I'm 'capable' of doesn't matter; I'm capable of doing whatever I set my mind to. 'Aim higher' can mean many things to different people. I would say that I aimed high by knowing myself and knowing what I wanted to do and loving it."

Grace made me think hard about my expectations for my own children's college experience. It is common on college campuses for us to talk about the importance of "fit" (much more on that later). We often do it using high-minded language. But a truly authentic conversation holds open the possibility that a good college fit can have many different outcomes. Our kids may make collegiate choices we neither prefer nor understand. But as I pointed out to the parent who asked, "What if my daughter makes a bad choice?" the only bad choice is a thoughtless choice. Give your child and yourself the space and permission to explore. The college path they choose, the one that may provide them the best opportunity to shape and achieve their dreams and aspirations, may not be what you think.

College Isn't What It Used to Be

Leafy green campuses dotted with stately buildings and gleaming athletic fields. Bright-eyed young people fresh from high school, hustling from dorm room to classroom to library. Intimate places where students, faculty, and staff know each other well. Community rituals that define moments and passages, like homecoming and commencement. Residence halls, dining halls, and roommates. Saturday afternoon football games. Backpacks, lectures, and labs. Caps, gowns, and four-year degrees.

For decades, these images have shaped perceptions about the typical or traditional college experience. I have the excellent fortune to work at institutions described by those images. It is wonderful. However, schools like mine do not even begin to capture the enormous variety of choices that characterize the college experience today. A brief walk through history reveals the incredible shape-shifting form of American higher education, changes that reflect the increasing social, economic, and cultural diversity of our nation.

Before World War II, college lived beyond the experience of most people. Most had little access to it or little interest in it. Many had not even finished high school, and few needed a postsecondary education as a prerequisite for a job. In 1940, less than 5 percent of all Americans had completed four or more years of college.[2] Things began to change rapidly after the war, but even as late as 1960, the nation's two thousand colleges and universities enrolled fewer than four million students.

The number of people going to college and the number of institutions serving them have exploded over the past fifty years. Students now have more choices than ever. Today nearly forty-six hundred colleges and universities operate in the United States, 30 percent more than as recently as 1990. Those institutions enroll approximately twenty million students of all levels, ages, and abilities. By 2015, nearly seven in ten high school graduates nationally were enrolling in a college somewhere within one year of having completed high school.[3] By any reckoning, the change has been extraordinary.

The growth reflects the changing role and place of higher education in American life. In a relatively short period of time—less than fifty years—a college experience has become much more important both to our economy and to people. The birth and boom of the commercial Internet by the end of the 1990s, the ascendance and dominance of a highly integrated world economy, and a steady move away from an industrial economic base to one more heavily rooted in innovation and service each signaled a significant change in both the perceived and real value of postsecondary education.

Without doubt, the amount and pace of change in our lives has accelerated, often in unnerving ways.[4] No longer simply a nice-to-have experience, postsecondary education of some kind has now become a virtual necessity. The educational bar for successful participation in our modern society has risen. In just two generations, college has displaced high school as the threshold test for economic independence and sustainability. No signs suggest the clock will turn back.

It is perhaps ironic, or at least paradoxical, that colleges are branded as places that prepare people for the future at the same time they are caricatured as beholden to unchanging and even unyielding traditions stuck in the past. Tradition does in fact shape the experience at many institutions, but American colleges and universities have always responded to changing social, economic, and cultural demands for education. A remarkable intellectual, technical, and professional smorgasbord of choices characterizes contemporary higher education in the United States. The days of a curriculum limited to the Greek *trivium* (grammar, logic, and rhetoric) and *quadrivium* (arithmetic, geometry, music, and astronomy) passed long ago—though modernized versions of the Grecian roots of the liberal arts still form the educational foundation at many four-year colleges.

Pablo Picasso is widely credited with having said, "Everything you can imagine is real."[5] That sentiment surely could describe American higher education. The US Department of Education has for nearly forty years maintained a classification system to track and report fields of study at two-year, four-year, and specialized colleges and universities across the country. They routinely update the list to capture an amazingly wide spectrum of academic offerings.

The Classification of Instructional Programs, the formal name of the system, now cites nearly nineteen hundred different academic programs and specialties.[6] The list includes traditional humanities and social science programs familiar to many people, like English, political science, art, and history, as well as classic scientific fields, like biology, chemistry, physics, and mathematics, among many others. The list also includes highly specialized professional and technical fields like avionics maintenance technology, blasting (focused on the use of explosives in the construction industry), and wine stewardship (sommeliers have to learn somewhere). More contemporary and sometimes exotic-sounding degree programs include Ayurvedic medicine (a system of holistic health care), pet grooming, yoga, and casino management.

Even a quick perusal of the list makes it eminently clear that any academic program you can imagine likely is offered for degree on a college campus somewhere. On the one hand, the vast number of choices is dizzying, the list of specializations alone running pages long. On the other, the choices reflect the extraordinary opportunities students now have to find and pursue a program that best suits their interests, skills, and aspirations. American colleges and universities today offer more academic choices than at any time in their history, and the list of programs will continue to change and grow as the demand for new knowledge and new skills changes and grows. We are constrained only by the limits of our imagination.

More than academic programs have changed. The ways we understand and define colleges themselves also have evolved. Although the words *college* and *university* still are commonly used to describe most postsecondary institutions in the United States, the meaning of the terms has expanded and blurred. Colleges today come in all shapes, sizes, and forms. No single school or type of school can claim the mantle of "typical." Colleges may be public, private not-for-profit, or private for-profit institutions, reflecting not only different management structures but often different purposes. They may provide a principally residential experience or be entirely nonresidential, in some cases having no physical campus at all. They may present expansive (the marketing term of art is *comprehensive*) missions, offering a mind-boggling number of degrees and serving students of all levels, types, abilities, and ages. Or colleges may be highly specialized, focusing on just one discipline or program.

Even seemingly straightforward descriptive terms like *two-year* or *four-year* college in many cases no longer accurately convey the scope of activity at schools operating under those descriptors. Many colleges founded as two-year schools now offer both associate's and bachelor's degrees, as well as a variety of nondegree certifications, broadly expanding their appeal. Among four-year colleges, many that historically had served only undergraduate students have extended their reach to provide graduate, nonresidential, and nondegree education of all kinds. Try as we might to develop a simple and comprehensive way to capture *college*, we can't. Though sometimes confusing, that's actually good news for students. They have more ways and places than ever to experience college.

College isn't what it used to be. And neither are students. It remains true that most undergraduate students in the United States are under age 24, but colleges and universities today commonly provide a multigenerational experience inside and outside of the classroom. As the number and type of institutions have changed, so too have the kinds of students enrolling as undergraduates.

A half-century or so ago, when people talked about college, they typically described an experience for young people. In 1950, 85 percent of all college students in the United States were under age 25.[7] For the next twenty years, that didn't change much. As recently as 1970, nearly nine in ten US undergraduates, and a similar proportion of community college students, were aged 18 to 24. Times have changed. Public and private four-year colleges and universities now enroll nearly two million undergraduate students older than age 24. Nontraditional-aged students, who are anything but nontraditional anymore on many American campuses, collectively represent 20 percent of total enrollment at four-year colleges and universities. Fully one-quarter of those nontraditional-aged students are over age 40, a remarkable change in just two generations—and a clear reflection of the evolving value and importance of lifelong learning. At community colleges, students over age 24 now make up 35 percent of all students.[8] College in America is no longer the nearly exclusive province of the young. New students today are likely to encounter peers of all ages and experiences in class and on campus, creating richer opportunities to encounter different views, perspectives, and life experiences.

I do not have a crystal ball to predict the future of higher education. What I know for certain, though, is that, like everything else, it will not remain the same. Yogi Berra was right: "The future ain't what it used to be."[9] New types of schools and programs, serving students of all ages and abilities, will continue to emerge as US higher education becomes more entrepreneurial, challenging and reshaping our historic understanding of college—and offering our children an even wider variety of choices and opportunities to prepare them for futures we cannot yet imagine.

Is College Worth It?

Each fall, nearly three million new students show up on the campuses of American colleges and universities. Today, nearly seven in ten high school graduates enroll at a two-year or four-year college within one year of finishing high school, compared to less than half in 1980.[10] Some arrive confident and prepared to take on the world. Others wonder and fear whether they have made a good school choice or even the right choice to go to college at all. That so many enroll indicates the allure and promise of higher education. As parents, we shouldn't take the choice lightly or simply assume its value. It is completely fair to ask: Is college worth it? Take some time to reflect on that question, both alone and with your children.

I have for years bowled in a men's league in Cold Spring, Minnesota. I'm not a particularly good bowler, though my handicap score occasionally helps us out in Tuesday night league play. As it turns out, bowling alleys can also be useful places to learn. Every week I hear a lot about the comings and goings of our small town and gain insights into the concerns and issues of families in our community. It's a useful antidote to the sometimes rarefied air and language of a college campus. A few years ago, a casual conversation about college with a new teammate turned into a long rant by him about how postsecondary education did not prepare anyone for anything. He had not gone to college and colorfully described how he would never send his children to college. At the time, I chalked up his soliloquy as bowling alley chatter. Random banter and rants often typify league night, and there was no need to spoil a good game with an argument. But to leave it at that would miss the point. The sentiment he expressed has some traction today, particularly as the cost of college has risen.

Concerns about the value of college extend well beyond bowling alley chatter. Responding to a comment about the need for people to have a college degree, Peter Thiel, PayPal founder and entrepreneur, offered a sharp criticism. "This vision is commonplace, but it implies a bleak future where everyone must work harder just to stay in place," he said in a *Washington Post* op-ed, "and it's just not true. Nothing forces us to funnel students into a tournament that bankrupts the losers and turns the winners into conformists. But that's what will happen until we start questioning whether college is our only option."[11] Thiel offered two broad criticisms of higher education. He first asserted that the college experience adds little value. Smart students were smart to begin with and in any case, while in college, they invest too much time in social experiences that add no value. Next, he labeled the admission system as a zero-sum tournament that favors the already elite and shuts out everyone else. And even then he described the winners as doing little more than perpetuating old ways of thinking and working. Thiel's view is remarkably dystopian and narrow and unfortunately provides no guidance to anyone about an alternative. If not college, then what, and for whom?

Still, colleges cannot simply ignore or wish away Thiel's critique and others like it. They need to think carefully about outcomes and find a better and more compelling way of expressing them to students and families. But the notion of value extends beyond economic outcomes and also has to recognize motivation. Why do students go to college? Is it simply a herd response driven by an economic impulse? Or do they seek other outcomes or values?

As it turns out, our kids are more thoughtful and sophisticated than we sometimes recognize or credit when it comes to thinking about the value of college. Economic conditions and cultural trends notwithstanding, the key reasons new students identify for going to college have not changed much over the last twenty years. To be sure, they frequently cite access to better jobs and the opportunity to make more money as important to their choice, expectations often shaped by their parents and the economic marketplace. In the fall of 2016, about 85 percent of all first-time new students attending four-year colleges in the United States indicated that the opportunity to "get a better job" was a very important factor in their decision to go to college. Nearly three-quarters also cited the opportunity to "make more money" as very important.

But as they head off to college, students think about and care about more than money and economic returns. They consistently express strong interest in cognitive and developmental outcomes. Half of all new college students nationally indicate that they expect college to make them more cultured people, and more than eight in ten cite the opportunity to "learn more about things that interest me" as very important. Three-quarters also point to the importance of opportunities to gain a general education and appreciation of ideas. Contrary to what we might assume about the allure of economic self-interest, the importance students place on learning actually trumps the importance of making more money.

In terms of life objectives after college, most new students describe "being very well off financially" as very important or essential. However, students historically and consistently also have cited raising a family and helping others in need as key life goals. Curiously, perhaps gratifyingly, students typically don't go to college simply to please their parents. They make the choice to suit their own purposes. In 2016, only about one-third of all new students nationally identified pleasing their family as an important reason for going to college.[12] I find all of these results heartening. On balance, our children have a far deeper interest in the broad value of education than we often do as adults, interests representative of the idealism and optimism of youth. Those values will shape not only the college choices they make but also their academic choices and, ultimately, their life experiences.

Students go to college for a variety of often highly optimistic reasons. But what happens as a result of having gone to college? How are we to think about the outcomes of a college education for our children? The first thing to keep in mind is that our daughters and sons are themselves the primary input to their own output or outcome; the more they put into it, the more they get out of it. From the vantage point of students, they control or own three conditions essential to their educational experience and outcomes: their aspiration (what they seek to do), their preparation (what they are prepared to do), and their motivation (their willingness to work hard to make use of their preparation to achieve their aspiration). Those three factors influence where they will go to college, how they will experience college, and what will happen to them after college.

That's the good news: Our daughters and sons have an opportunity to shape a significant portion of their own destiny. In the end, their success demands that they fully own their education and their choices. That may be hard to imagine from the vantage point of a parent of a 12-year-old, but it's what makes parenting of teens and young adults so interesting (and occasionally confounding and exasperating!).

But other forces come in to play as well, forces not so amenable to individual control that add uncertainty and risk: the economic demand for certain skills or experiences, which are not static; the cultural demand for certain experiences or values, also dynamic; the quality of preparation, academic and nonacademic; and, not least of all, though often overlooked, luck. It is good to be in the right place at the right time. Those forces demand a level of realism that can be hard on us as parents. Hard work does not always turn out the way we imagine it should. Our young adult children are required to develop the skills of flexibility and resilience, especially during times of sweeping economic, social, and cultural change. Perhaps we can take some solace in the notion that these forces were as important and influential when we were young as they are now.

Having identified the broad forces that influence the outcomes of a college education, let's cut to the economic chase: Is a college education still worth it? In economic terms, absolutely (on average—an important caveat). In their report, "The Rising Cost of *Not* Going to College," the Pew Research Center, a venerable nonpartisan research organization, noted the following:

> On virtually every measure of economic well-being and career attainment—from personal earnings to job satisfaction to the share employed full time—young college graduates are outperforming their peers with less education. And when today's young adults are compared with previous generations, the disparity in economic outcomes between college graduates and those with a high school diploma or less formal schooling has never been greater in the modern era.[13]

The greatest economic returns accrue to those who complete college, no matter the level of college they finish (though incomes also typically rise with each successive level of degree attainment). Starting college is a great first step but not a sufficient final step for economic purposes. Through the prism of economics, the primary value of college lies in completion and the attainment of a degree or certificate— important to keep in mind as college completion rates significantly lag college enrollment rates. Many are called; far fewer complete. Without doubt, the economic costs and consequences associated with inability to complete can be very high.

Data on the income and employment outcomes associated with college completion point to a compelling advantage. In 2015, the average earnings of young people (those aged 25 to 29) who earned a bachelor's degree totaled $50,000, more than 50 percent greater than the average for similar-aged young adults who either only completed high school or went to college but did not complete a degree.[14] The educational income advantage gained at a young age piles up over a lifetime. A study by the Brookings Institution's Hamilton Project found that median earnings of those who completed a bachelor's degree were higher than the median for those who earned only a high school diploma at career entry, midcareer, and end of career for all academic majors.[15] Four-year college graduates will earn an average of more than $1 million over the course of their careers (though cumulative earnings vary considerably by degree and occupational choice). I have long believed that we place too much emphasis on the first job after college—though perhaps that reflects our fear as parents that our sons and daughters will become permanent residents of our basements. "First job" almost never equals "best chance" or "last chance" for economic self-sufficiency. Even among the lowest-earning majors, a significant income growth often occurs within the first five years of employment, a powerful indication of the mobility and opportunity that educational attainment affords.

Though colleges and universities clearly contribute to labor markets, they do not control those markets. So when we think about post-college employment, we need to think less about guarantees and more about probabilities. Here, as with income returns, the economic results are unambiguous: the probability of employment rises with successive levels of educational attainment. The unemployment rate for young bachelor's degree holders typically is half the overall unemployment rate, a relationship that has held through good economic times and bad.[16] More importantly, college graduates are not simply less likely to be unemployed, they are much more likely to report working. Labor force participation rates—which measure the percentage of the population that is actually working or seeking work—indicate a clear divide for those who have completed college versus those who have not. Today, approximately three-quarters of all people with a bachelor's degree or higher report being part of the labor force (the overwhelming majority of them employed) compared to fewer than six in ten of those with no education beyond high school. Put another way, almost half of all Americans over age 25 who earned only a high school diploma are not working, compared to fewer than three in ten of those who earned a bachelor's degree or higher.[17]

Without doubt, in today's American economy, the best chance of finding sustainable, higher-paying work comes with pursuing and completing college. Georgetown University's Center on Education and the Workforce projected that by 2020, nearly two-thirds of all jobs in the United States would require postsecondary education or training beyond high school.[18] Whether all of those jobs will utilize all of the skills a college education delivers is an open question. What is not, though, is that most employers will continue to expect some kind of college education as a minimum expectation for job consideration and advancement. That outcome is not hard to imagine. During the last years of the twentieth century, with the birth and boom of the Internet and the advent of a truly integrated and interdependent global economy, higher education became a different kind of good or experience. No longer a luxury experience, a college education of some kind has become a necessity experience, now required for access to the middle class and the hope of economic self-sufficiency. In fewer than fifty years, college has displaced high school as the threshold test and expectation for economic independence and success.

Given the economic returns, it comes as no surprise that college graduates themselves typically describe their education as having paid off. Survey research by the Pew Research Center found that more than nine in ten adults who have earned a bachelor's degree or more report that their education has paid off (or they expect it to pay off) in relation to what their family paid for it. The results were consistent across all majors, all types of schools, and all age groups.[19]

Each year, my office surveys our young graduates three years after earning their bachelor's degree—long enough out of college for them to have launched but close enough to ensure a contemporary recollection of their experience (nostalgia is a powerful diluter of images for those of us who are considerably older!). Among other things, we ask our young graduates two key questions about value: If you could start college over, would you choose us again, and did the value of the education you received justify what your family paid for it? The results don't change much from year to year. More than 80 percent each year indicate that the value of their experience justified its cost, and more than 90 percent say they would choose us again. As you explore your children's college options, look at the economic returns of its graduates but also ask broader questions about the value its graduates cite. What kinds of benefits do the college's graduates describe for having attended the school? More than just overall satisfaction rates (too simple), look for ways the college has added value to the postgraduate life of their alumni. Colleges and universities should be able to provide that information. If they can't provide it, you also will have learned a great deal about what they know (or don't know) about their experience.

One final and important admonition. Not all results are created equally. A college degree does not *guarantee* a particular economic outcome, a fact often confused in popular media and a source of great anxiety for parents and students alike. Data describing average salaries or average employment impart important and powerful information. But they can only describe what is or has been for a group of people, not what will be for individuals looking forward. As all financial prospectuses are required to report, past performance is not a guarantee of future returns. So do not hesitate to ask good and probing questions about outcomes throughout your child's college search. At the same time, be wary of unrealistic expectations—your own and your child's. Your daughter or son will have their own experience, shaped by their own abilities and choices and the context of their own time. Remember that you were 18 once, too.

TWO

School Matters

Watch your thoughts, they become your beliefs. Watch your beliefs, they become your words. Watch your words, they become your actions. Watch your actions, they become your habits. Watch your habits, they become your character.
—**Vince Lombardi**

✉ **From Matt Malatesta, Vice President for Admissions, Financial Aid and Enrollment, Union College, New York**

Dear Parents,

My family today could be described by an old baseball metaphor: our bases are loaded. We have three children who span the ages of 7 to 15 at three different levels of school: elementary, middle, and high school. Clearly, we are playing a long game, now still in the early innings. As the dean of admissions at a highly selective college, I am tempted to think I have a game plan set, all the answers and pathways in place. Tempted, but I would be wrong. My wife and I don't have it all figured out, but we try to make a little progress every day.

As an admissions dean, thinking continuously about college represents something of a professional hazard. I try not to deliberate about my children's college prospects every day, but those thoughts do creep in occasionally. I recently attended a conference at a university and found myself handing my high school daughter a map of the campus and a brochure upon my return. Alas, the college search had begun for this unwitting ninth grader. The next day, I learned that my son had received the honorific "Super Student" at his middle school. I had taught middle school earlier in my career, so I knew it may simply have meant that he did not glue anyone to a desk during the term. Still, I found myself making a point of formally shaking his hand and congratulating him on his achievement. As he mumbled, "Whatever, Dad," I was thinking, "Stay on the right path, Son." The next morning, I mentioned my son's accomplishment to his younger sister, both to shock her that one of her chief tormentors could do some good in the world and also to model the way for her.

I often find the advice my wife and I give our children about college to be simple (not the kind of wisdom I expected to provide before we had children). We encourage our younger kids to work hard and challenge themselves. We've had an adage in our family for years: "Good kids get good stuff." Simply put, if you work hard and behave (at least most of the time), good things will happen. Perhaps not too deep, but it works. For our high schooler, the message focuses on life balance. When she recently asked me if she should add another class to her schedule, I asked her if she likes lunch. She likes lunch. The two conflicted. She chose lunch. Good choice.

Without doubt, worry and stress often stand in the way of student success at all levels—elementary, middle, high school, and even college. We encourage our three children to challenge themselves appropriately, to learn how to push themselves, and to learn to try consistently to do their best. However, even as they do that, we want them to embrace other important family rules, like be safe, have fun, and be kind. If my wife and I succeed with those seemingly simple or basic practices, we can move on to harder things!

Kids need to learn how to learn, to challenge themselves, to live a balanced life, to have fun—not how to get into college or a particular college. Strong colleges and universities across the country are interested in enrolling students from a variety of educational backgrounds and with different levels of academic achievement. Admission is not the goal or the endgame. The more important question for our children is, "Are you ready to stretch yourself and continue to grow once in college?" I'm hopeful that with occasional prodding, my children will later describe their college years as a home run experience!

✉ **From Karen Cooper, Director of Financial Aid, Stanford University, California**

Dear Parents,

My husband and I are the proud parents of three young adults with their own unique personalities, motivations, dreams, and desires. Each has taken an entirely different approach to education.

I've spent most of my career as a financial aid administrator at Stanford University. Stanford has been part of our lives since our oldest child was nine months old. In my professional life, I've experienced parents who are deeply involved in every aspect of their children's lives and perhaps a bit too personally invested in their children's success in an increasingly competitive admission process. I decided early on that I didn't want to be a managing-partner parent and would instead let my children take the lead in decisions related to their paths after high school. We worked to introduce our kids to many different kinds of postsecondary opportunities while being clear that the final decision was theirs.

With the wisdom of today, I would describe our laid-back approach as having had varying degrees of success. I'm happy to say that all three of our children are a pleasure to be around, have a good work ethic, and enjoy helping others. I love the young adults they have become. That said, their paths to and through college have been as unique as each of them. The oldest spoiled us; she's always had a plan and marched through a bachelor's and master's degree, as well as the start of her career, with barely a pause. The older of her two younger brothers had a terrific high school sports career, but academics wasn't a priority for him. Since finishing high school, he has "sampled" a variety of community colleges in our area and finally realized that he has more to offer than the jobs he's been working demand of him. He now is on track to finish an associate's degree to complement his personal trainer's license. I don't know if he'll ever give himself the luxury of being a full-time student, but he seems to be happiest and at his best as a part-time student with a job to keep him busy. Our younger son (and youngest child) struggled with a traditional high school experience, making his first year of college a challenge for him. We've agreed to give him the time he needs to figure out his next steps. We know that it is more important for him to take the time to make good decisions for himself than for his mom to be able to brag about his accomplishments (although I do expect amazing things from him—watch out!).

It is important for all of us as parents to keep in mind who our children are, who they are becoming, and the relationships we have with them. The college choice is not the sole driver of our children's development or success; they learn from all of their experiences. Keep the final goal in mind. It's ultimately not about admittance to a college you can brag about but rather the development of fully functioning, contributing members of society that you want to spend time with at family reunions!

✉ **From Renee Bischoff, Director of College Counseling, Hawken School, Ohio, and Rick Bischoff, Vice President for Enrollment, Case Western Reserve University, Ohio**

Dear Parents,

Over our careers in education, we have been called upon as professionals to provide advice to thousands and thousands of students and their parents. Our mantra as parents has been, "We are trying to raise a great 35-year-old, not a great college applicant or even a great college student." That often is harder than you might think for two parents who have spent most of their adult lives working with students in the transition from high school to college. We often have wondered if we would be able to follow our own advice when the time came for our son to go through the process. We won't know how it all turns out for a few more years, but we have certainly learned that it is difficult. We know how important various pieces of his early experience are to the college process, and it is tempting to become an overbearing, micromanaging parent trying to maximize the college prize at the expense of all else. We work hard to resist that temptation.

We saw middle school as a time for our son to learn independence, self-sufficiency, and self-advocacy. At the end of the day, middle school grades matter much less than the skills students learn to master in those formative years. In the spring of our son's eighth grade, we sat down with him and had a conversation about our expectations for high school. Those expectations explicitly did not include straight A's. Yes, we wanted him to work hard and do his best. But we also expected him to be positive and respectful to his teachers and classmates and to be engaged in his school community. The latter two points were as important as the first. We made it clear that his school day would not end with the end of his classes and the ringing of the school bell. We expected him to find something to engage his time after school that involved the community. We were less concerned with the particular activity he chose but impressed on him that he was going to do something.

By choosing not to focus on his grades, grade point average, or class rank, we know that we may be opting out of hyper-selective college choices. We are comfortable with the potential outcome. Lots of great colleges are out there. And in any case, even in our house, he has picked up most of his college knowledge from ESPN! We have been careful not to malign or preemptively categorize schools as "good" or "bad." We don't know where he will ultimately enroll (and we don't indulge in speculation with each other or with other parents), but we want to set the expectation now that wherever he chooses—"name brand" school or not—it should be a place he can be excited about and proud to attend. We have always emphasized that college is a place to take off, not a place to land. Further, we have always maintained that there is not one path to further education. We started talking to our son when he was in seventh grade about the opportunity to pursue a gap year after high school so that he doesn't assume that everyone must follow the same linear path. We hope he will follow his own path.

Our professional experience no doubt influences our parenting. We value real-world learning and experiences because we expect our son to be a thoughtful, contributing member of society. We care that our son is knowledgeable about political, social, and economic issues. We pay attention to the news and discuss current issues. Not quizzes over dinner, but rather conversations about what is going on in America because it is his home and he will be able to vote in a few years. It is important that he learn to form his own opinions and argue them with evidence and conviction.

We also believe in the value of pitching in at home. A refrain often heard in our house is, "Are you a part of the family?" From an early age, doing his laundry, helping in the yard, caring for his pets, and engaging in the business of operating a household have been important. We do not see ourselves as concierge parents. Though our son grumbled about our rules and chores when he was younger, he is grateful for the independence he enjoys now. We can leave him home for the day knowing that he will manage a sizable list of jobs while we are gone. There is great value in contributing to a family, and he feels good about what he does around the house (he's very proud of his lawn management!). Lest you worry that he has no fun, we totally support unscheduled downtime. The biggest lesson we learned from elementary school is that too many activities fail to encourage a passionate interest. Our rule is that when he makes a commitment, he needs to stick with it for at least a year. This has resulted in a few deeply meaningful activities and plenty of time to do other things.

We see being a good community member as paramount to a positive college experience. We want to set the expectation that an education is more than classes so that he finds ways to engage beyond the classroom in college, whether in sports, service, outdoor activities, or academically oriented organizations. We have intentionally tried to give him experiences that are challenging and opportunities to fail so that he won't have to face those experiences (and emotions) for the first time while in college. Failure and struggle are important. Working through them builds resilience—the "grit" everyone talks about—and helps children start to identify what is most important in their lives.

Our son has learned, through academic and athletic struggles, that the world often is not fair. We have seen him manage his frustration by working through challenges on his own. It is hard as a parent to watch when you could simply fix it for him. Although we make no claim to perfection, by providing him the space and guidance for taking on his own issues, we have supported a pattern of behavior leading to independence and self-confidence.

We definitely experience the same challenges common to parents today, which include screen time, video games, and procrastination.

A teenage boy operates in different ways from his middle-aged parents (especially his type A mother). We strive to set reasonable limits, while also letting our son discover that there are opportunity costs when it comes to time management. We also know that he is growing in his abilities to organize his life (work, sports, and downtime). These executive-functioning skills take time to develop, and though the process of learning these skills may result in a few disappointments along the way, we hope it leads to a more independent and confident adult. In the process, we want to have a positive relationship with our son, who is a funny, kind, goofy, messy, soccer-obsessed, starving, dog-loving, and curious young man. We think too many parents shoot for the moon (college) and miss getting to know their child along the way. We know that the time goes by far too quickly, and we want to look back and not have every memory tinged with the idea of college.

Our goal is to raise a great 35-year-old, and college is likely to be a part of that journey. We define "great" broadly, with the single most important measure of our success as parents being the adult relationship we have with our son. That's way more important than where he goes to college.

The Long and Winding Road

My mother was the only child of Italian immigrants who believed deeply in the value of education for their daughter. They viewed her education not simply as *a* way up, but as the *best* way up. My father was an early beneficiary of the GI Bill, which created opportunities for veterans that had not existed prior to the law's introduction. A generation later my parents sent my three brothers and me off to college—an educational march that lasted nine years from start to finish, culminating in all of us earning college degrees. We were not wealthy, so our parents did it the hard way—through saving and sacrifice, always encouraging us to pursue our educational dreams. I had only a vague idea then about the sacrifices they made for us. Now with four children of my own, I think often about my parents and the wisdom and guidance they provided us and what that commitment yielded.

My own children are like the rings on my family's tree of life. Occasionally I look back and reflect on how quickly infancy moved to toddlerhood, then to school age, and ultimately to young adulthood and independence. How come they get older but we seemingly do not (a delusion, to be sure)? My wife has spent her entire professional life working with children and parents. She began her career as an elementary school teacher. More recently, she has served as a parent educator in early childhood family education programs. Over a career working with young children and their parents, she has experienced moments of great joy and hope, as well as moments of tremendous frustration and even sadness. She learned long ago that a child's future educational prospects typically are not shaped during the high school years but rather much earlier, often before a child even begins formal schooling. Her early childhood parent curriculum regularly included a financial aid night to introduce parents with toddlers to college costs and help them to prepare for postsecondary enrollment later. I'm sure it seemed a foggy future to most at the time. But as any parent with children who have just finished high school will tell you, eighteen years go by very quickly.

When should you start preparing for college in earnest? Admission professionals frequently get questions like that. Matt Malatesta's advice is spot on: college admission is not an end, it is a means. It starts as soon as we begin to teach and guide our children—which means, in practice, as soon as they are born. As parents, we need to encourage our kids to explore, challenge, and learn to the best of their ability— while recognizing ourselves that neither perfection nor prizes are the objective or purpose. Students that come to college knowing how to learn, how to live a balanced life, how to challenge themselves, and even how to have fun most often have the most successful and satisfying college experiences regardless of the schools they choose to attend. They are prepared for the rigors and joys of life, not just for the rigors and sometimes angst of college admission.

The formal college search process occurs over a relatively short period of time. Most colleges and universities today begin reaching out to students in or around the tenth grade, when—ready or not—they send out the first admission marketing pieces. The process intensifies over the next twenty-four to thirty-six months as postal mailboxes and email inboxes of students sometimes fill to their capacity or beyond. As students apply to college, those schools examine their high school records and applications with the same intensity of an avid baseball fan reading a box score. They comb through essays and personal statements, transcripts and board scores, letters of recommendation and commendation in an extremely short period of time to gauge not only preparation and readiness, but potential and fit. You need to know that all colleges and universities dream about large and fully qualified admission pools. Some will succeed in reaching their goals, others not.

But preparing for college—or, more accurately, preparation for a successful college experience—begins long before the first colorful brochure reaches a student's home. A study sponsored by the Minnesota Private College Research Foundation found that only about one in ten parents of middle school students in Minnesota described seventh or eighth grade as too early to start planning for college.[1] More than half said it was *too late*. More than anything else, parents of pre-high school–age children craved reassurance. They wanted help identifying ways to save for college and to prepare their children academically for college.

As someone who spent a considerable amount of time in birthing centers awaiting the arrival of each of our four children, I believe early thinking and planning can yield valuable results—and help reduce stress and anxiety later. But does that require our children to begin preparing for the SAT as preschoolers or that we should begin gathering college materials when our children are in their early elementary years? Emphatically, no. Does it mean, however, that we should pay attention to our children's academic development and offer great encouragement and guidance along the way? Decidedly, yes.

Grow, Show, Go

Though they have grown up together and been subjected to a similar set of home and family values and rules (mostly willingly), my four children are quite different from each other. One is highly organized and driven, one is flexible and imaginative, one is fiercely independent and studious, and one is artistic and creative. Those terms capture only a part of who they are, of course, but they do broadly describe the ways each is distinctly his or her own person. Their shared gene pool and family experiences notwithstanding, my wife and I have had to adapt our parenting and our expectations to their unique abilities and interests. While that makes obvious sense in theory, in practice it can be difficult, particularly when it comes to guiding their educational development. It is easy to project the learning experiences and aspirations of one child, often the oldest, onto the others. However, neither one size nor one experience fits all. That can be a hard lesson to learn.

College isn't something that suddenly or magically happens after the senior year of high school. It's the culmination of a long and sometimes winding path that begins when our children are very young. The path includes five basic (and easy to remember) steps that roll out more or less sequentially, with parents playing an important role at each stage:

- *Awareness* of college as an option and opportunity. Families for whom college is a multigenerational experience or simply an expectation typically don't think about this much. Past experience often shapes their understanding and expectation. My own children have grown up on a college campus. They have had some experience of how and why colleges work. My wife and I have never explicitly told our children they had to go to college, but our kids have grown up expecting college to be an important part of their future. But for students who would be the first in their family to attend college, this can hardly be assumed. Awareness and interest for first-generation students must be built from the ground floor. If you know somebody currently enrolled in college, or have friends whose children are enrolled, ask them about their postsecondary experience. What is it like? What do they hope someday to do or be? Simple questions, to be sure, but questions for which the answers will be as varied and interesting as the people you ask. Mentors and role models play an outsized role helping children and young people develop images of college and life beyond.

- An *aspiration* to pursue a college education. Simply being aware that colleges exist and create important life opportunities is not by itself sufficient to assume interest and a decision to someday enroll. Students ultimately must aspire to attend college and pursue a degree. They have to develop an understanding of its value for themselves. This often is a far steeper hill to climb than many imagine. I have found that it's especially difficult for parents who have assumed their children will go to college only to find themselves disappointed, perhaps even ashamed or angry, when their children do not reach the same conclusion. Aspiration generally cannot be imposed. It comes from talking, not stalking, and is nurtured and guided over many years. And even then, our children may confound us.

- Some level of *academic achievement* (minimally including high school completion). Teenagers throughout the ages have had to listen to their parents lecture them about the importance of doing well in school. Just as frequently, teenagers have responded with rolling eyes. Teens seem to have perfected the art of practiced indifference. It turns out, though, the advice to do well in school is sound. Good grades and good academic choices can open a world of college options and, depending on the schools to which your children apply, significant scholarship opportunities. That doesn't mean straight A's or perfect SAT scores—academic requirements and expectations vary widely among the nation's thousands of colleges—but rather that you should encourage your children to develop good academic habits, preferably when they are young and learning is new and fun. Good habits of effort and responsibility developed at an early age pay off with a commitment to achievement much later.

- Completing an application for college *admission*. Although this seems obvious enough, it often is a difficult step for students. Not so much the act of applying for admission but rather the affirmative act of choosing a group of colleges to which to apply. Submitting an application for admission requires forethought, some level of research, and commitment. It in many ways represents the culmination of awareness, aspiration, and achievement. My two children who have been through the process clearly experienced a sense of pride, relief, and anxiety when they hit "send" on their computers to submit their college applications. On the one hand, it's an exhilarating act of independence and forward movement. On the other, it represents a step into the new and unknown. Though sometimes perceived as little more than a hoop-jumping bureaucratic task, the application represents the primary tool for evaluating students for admission. Encourage your daughter or son to take it seriously.

- An understanding of *affordability*. I'll talk much more about this later, but national research clearly indicates that young people today are as concerned as their parents about affordability and the ability of their families to pay for college. Family conversations about money often are uncomfortable, particularly when they focus not on opportunity but limits. As parents, we want to provide as much as we can for our children, but that by necessity involves staking out boundaries. Before your daughter or son begins the college search and selection process, it's important that you understand your sense of value and your financial limits, as well as the financial commitment you expect from them. College may be the single largest expense your family incurs, second only to a home (and, if you have more than one child, perhaps more than that). Do not select a college without a clear understanding of your ability to pay for it.

The College Board describes the five steps more simply as grow, show, and go. That's an elegant and appealing way to cast it. Learning is made up of a series of milestones, each providing a foundation for the next. It is cumulative and has no end. Though the dictionary notes otherwise, learning is not a noun. It most definitely is a verb, an action. And it's an action built on practice. Greg Walker is a vice president for the College Board. A former school principal, teacher, and Division I college athlete, he deeply understands the value of practice for learning and achievement. "From the time our children were small, my wife and I embraced the notion of homework because we understood the importance of reinforcement through practice. Practice is essential in every aspect of life. It may not equate to perfection, but it does lead to improvement and that was always the goal, the ability to do better."

Greg noted that his children, not unexpectedly, pushed back on the call to practice. "But as our kids got older, they pushed back less," he said. "They got used to practicing. Even in the hazy days of summer, my wife made sure their brains worked." Walker is an emphatic believer in the value and importance of practice as preparation for college, and he impressed that on his own children during their school years.

"The purpose of practice is preparation. Just as an athlete prepares for competition or a musician prepares for a concert, a student who intends to go to college should prepare for college success," Greg said. "Challenging coursework and homework served as a foundation in planting the seed for college in our family. All parents want their children to be prepared for success, and we worked to make sure our daughter and sons would be ready to excel."

Walker's advice is both heartfelt and smart. Each step of education paves the way for the next. Demanding perfection creates unsustainable, damaging pressure for students. We often see the effects of that kind of pressure soon after those students arrive on campus, especially when they experience their first less-than-an-A grade. But encouraging the practice of learning—even a love of learning—beginning when kids are young will expand their collegiate opportunities, will prepare them to excel in college, and ultimately and best of all, will enrich their lives.

Alphabets and Acronyms

Education, at all levels, is a remarkably jargon-laden enterprise. We seem to relish and feast on an alphabet soup of shorthand labels and acronyms to describe programs and experiences. It is a language all its own, and one never fully mastered because new labels and acronyms appear as quickly as old ones fade. Acronyms and alphabet programs and tests define much of the college preparation process, each serving a particular purpose or group of students. They include:

- *AP (Advanced Placement).* AP courses, designed by the College Board and offered at secondary schools around the country, provide students with opportunities to take rigorous college-level courses while in high school. The courses are offered in a wide variety of disciplines and culminate with an exam, administered nationally. Individual high schools choose which AP courses they want to offer their students. Colleges and universities across the country offer credit, advanced curricular placement, or both to students who earn a qualifying score on their AP exams. Advanced credit and placement practices vary by college, and sometimes within a college, so it's best to ask any institution your daughter or son considers about how they recognize AP course-work. Millions of students across the country take AP courses each year.

- *IB (International Baccalaureate).* The International Baccalaureate is a nonprofit educational foundation offering programs of study at both the primary and secondary school levels. The IB Diploma Programme, offered at the high school level, is a two-year curriculum comprising six academic areas. Like AP, the IB program is rigorous and designed to prepare students for successful college experiences (not only in the United States but also globally). The International Baccalaureate foundation must approve schools offering IB programs. IB courses are recognized by colleges and universities throughout the country.

- *CIS (College in School).* Unlike AP or IB, which are built on a nationally or internationally created curriculum, college in the classroom courses typically represent partnerships between high schools and a nearby college. The courses are presented as college-level and are offered on site at the high school. Secondary school teachers receive guidance and preparation from college faculty in the design and structure of the courses. CIS courses, one of many different types of dual enrollment opportunities, are offered in a growing number of schools. However, because they represent local school-college partnerships rather than a nationally adjudicated curriculum, it's important that you check with colleges in advance to determine if or how much CIS credit they will recognize for advanced curricular placement. In addition to college in the classroom arrangements, many schools allow (and sometimes encourage) students to dual-enroll in local community colleges or four-year colleges—an opportunity for students to take actual college courses and earn college credit. (Don't worry if your student's high school does not offer AP, IB, or CIS courses. It will not diminish their college prospects.)

- *SAT and ACT (neither is used any longer as an acronym, but both are college assessment exams).* Widely known, and occasionally feared by high school students everywhere, the SAT and ACT assessments are the preeminent college assessment exams today. Though somewhat different in composition, both exams share the common purpose of assessing college preparation and readiness. Many school districts around the country use one exam or the other to assess learning in high school—and more and more states require that all students take one of the tests. Most four-year colleges and universities continue to require prospective students to submit an entrance exam score with their application for admission, but a rising number describe themselves as "test optional," giving students the opportunity to choose whether they want to provide their test scores. Colleges use the exam scores for two basic purposes: as part of a student's admission portfolio to make an admit (or deny) decision and, for many, to determine eligibility for achievement-based scholarship awards. All colleges accept the results of either the SAT or the ACT entrance exam.

These represent only a few (albeit the best known and most widely used) of the precollege courses and assessments available to high school students today. Without doubt, the lines between high school and college have blurred in recent years—as more secondary schools offer college-level courses or as secondary students take courses at local universities or community colleges.

For students seeking admission to selective colleges and universities, Advanced Placement courses and college assessments have taken on almost mythical status, becoming for many less about learning and the assessment of learning and more an "I have to take this course or achieve this score to get in" experience. On the one hand, that outcome is understandable given the intensity of competition for the relatively few admission slots available at the nation's most selective institutions.

On the other, it's a distraction that has turned both the coursework and the exams into something more like a competitive achievement arms race. "How many advanced placement or college-level courses can I accumulate? How many times must I take the exam to reach the highest score I can?" The result may be less qualitative improvement in learning and a great deal more pressure on students already pressured to achieve.

Preparation, challenge, and learning ought to be the goals. Students today often are encouraged, sometimes cajoled, to take as many advanced courses and college preparatory courses as they can without any sense of what the collection of courses adds up to in terms of learning. The result too often is a constellation of coursework not clearly connected to either any particular college's general education requirements or to a particular disciplinary major (to say nothing of the student's strengths or interests). Colleges must share some of the blame. We offer too little guidance about how to approach these learning opportunities and what they mean (or might mean) upon arrival at college.

In a *New York Times* story that asked deans of admission about the college preparation advice and guidance they provide to their own children, Stuart Schmill, Dean of Admissions at the Massachusetts Institute of Technology, shared an important piece of wisdom:

> What I tell students, and my own kids, is that you don't have to take every advanced class. My high school daughter, for example, is taking advanced math and science courses but chose not to take advanced English and history. You should challenge yourself. For some students this might mean taking the most advanced classes, but it also might mean taking the most advanced classes appropriate for that student, and not spreading themselves too thin.

The *New York Times* article goes on to say that "applicants do not need to tick off a laundry list of engagement in every field, like art, music, sports."[2]

So should kids take advantage of these opportunities? The answer in general is yes. A qualified yes. On balance, advanced placement or dual credit coursework prepares students for success in college. But not all of the alphabet opportunities are the same; their rigor varies, and the course choices your son or daughter makes matter. Help your daughter or son understand their choices in a broader framework than "I need to do this to look good to a particular college." In other words, help them to unpack their motivations, interests, and aspirations. Are they interested in college-level courses because they enjoy the subject matter, or to learn something new, or to position themselves for greater success in college, or on the expectation that the coursework or assessment will count for college credit later? These clearly are not mutually exclusive choices, but motivation influences performance and progress. The bottom line is that none of this work—and it is hard work—should simply be worn as a merit badge. Students should pursue courses and activities throughout their elementary and high school years that not only challenge their ability (and one size definitely does not fit all when it comes to level of challenge) but more importantly that help them to develop both their skills and their aspirations. The end is not college admission. The end is a fulfilling and rewarding life.

More Than a List

At a lunch hosted by a community organization to celebrate the achievements of local students, I listened to a high school senior breathlessly and painstakingly recite a list of her scholastic and personal achievements and experiences. The list was long. But though she surely had much to be proud of, I couldn't help but wonder as I listened whether she viewed her list of accomplishments as anything more than a kind of scorecard of her life, a series of checked boxes of tasks completed. Her enthusiastic staccato tone notwithstanding, I wondered how much she cared about any of it or learned from any of it, or whether she had simply built a resume around a set of cues that told her (or her parents) that she needed to accumulate experiences, grades, and accolades to access the kind of college she desired. I could not tell—and I prefer to give her the benefit of the doubt—but it was nonetheless a moment to reflect on the call-and-response incentives and myths that shape the way many students think about college admissions today. My children attend a competitive high school. It's a familiar story.

The perfect college application is a myth. Even the most selective schools aren't looking for perfect students—and what defines the ideal would vary by school, in any case. There simply is no universal standard that defines a perfect application for all students. Do high school grades matter? Yes. Do the kinds of courses students take in high school matter? Yes. Do entrance exam scores matter? Often. Do school and nonschool activities and commitments—academic, artistic, athletic, volunteer—matter? Yes. Does any one thing or collection of things guarantee your son or daughter acceptance to a particular college? Typically, no. Mostly, colleges seek to enroll interesting, hopefully genuine people. We look for applications that convincingly reflect the talents, values, and true commitments of students.

Though admission requirements and review processes differ significantly among colleges, the poles that define how most schools evaluate prospective students can be framed along two distinct but related dimensions:

- *Preparation and promise.* How has a student demonstrated learning—in coursework, on entrance exams, or perhaps through curricular, extracurricular, or volunteer projects and activities? Irrespective of the grades, test scores, or achievements a student has accumulated, does she or he show promise to do more and develop further as a college student? Colleges ultimately are trying to address a question of paramount importance to them and to students: Is the student prepared to succeed at the college or university? Though it may not seem like it as you experience your son or daughter's college search, colleges are not in the business of student admission but rather student success. And that is not simply a standard to which colleges hold students but is one to which students and families should hold colleges.

- *Commitment and authenticity.* Has the student demonstrated an authentic and meaningful commitment to learning or to a specific activity? Can the student demonstrate how their achievements or activities have contributed to their personal growth or development? How does the student intend to make a difference to others, to their communities, or to the world? Has the student ever reached beyond their comfort zone? Has she or he demonstrated grit or resilience? The answers to these kinds of questions, much more difficult for schools to gather and evaluate, require reflection. However, they are important to many colleges because they allow them to move beyond consideration of what a student has done and toward a more complete picture of who they are and who they seek to become.

Eighteen years of parenting (including thirteen or more years of elementary and secondary schooling) seems like a long time—and in many ways it is. But to reduce the value or measurement of those years to lists or sterling exam scores or grades entirely misses the point of both learning and parenting. Steven Farmer, Vice Provost for Enrollment and Undergraduate Admissions at the University of North Carolina, Chapel Hill, said it most eloquently in a *New York Times* interview in 2016:

> My wife and I have tried to give our kids some air and room to breathe growing up. We never checked their homework or felt like their schooling was a family project. It was their life and their work—we provided guidance. In the end, our kids need our love more than they need our direction about college. If that direction gets in the way of the love, it's not helpful and it's not worth it.[3]

Preparation for college does, in fact, begin when our children are very young. But that doesn't mean test preparation courses at age 12 or unrealistic academic expectations and demands or admission visits in eighth grade. Instead, it is a process built on encouragement, attentiveness, and discovery. I offer four simple steps to guide the way:

1. *Talk with your kids* about school, their coursework, and their experiences. It's easy when they are young and excited about school. It becomes more challenging when they are teens and less interested in "How was your day?" banter. But it is important at every age. Support and encourage them, teaching them how to succeed, as well as how to develop the resilience required to survive and learn from failure. Their body language sometimes notwithstanding, kids of all ages actually care that we care and pay attention to them.

2. *Talk with teachers and school counselors* about your daughter or son's courses, both to understand how your students are progressing and to understand how their courses and course

sequencing help prepare them for a successful college experience later. Make academic choices that make sense both for your child and to you.

3. *Encourage your son or daughter to engage in academic, arts, athletic, or community service activities.* Not because this is what colleges look for, but rather because those activities help them develop and mature as people. They provide avenues for the development and expression of their talents and interests. My wife and I have always insisted that our children be involved in activities inside and outside of school. And we let them choose. As for how many, it's more important that they engage deeply in a few activities than superficially in many.

4. *Visit a college campus* when your children are young, not to assess it for future consideration but to get a sense of what colleges are like. Colleges of all types welcome guests. And on any given day, they host a buffet of academic, arts, cultural, and athletic events open to the public, many of them free or at low cost. One of the great privileges of working on a college campus is the opportunity to experience daily their vibrancy. They pulse with energy. My kids have grown up on campus, regularly attending athletic events, theater, films, and concerts. I wouldn't trade the experience—or the fun—for anything.

Parenthood is not a process of holding on but rather of preparing to let go, all the while trying to make sure that the children we let go are prepared. And the guidance, nurturing, and role modeling we provide make all the difference in the world.

Dear Parents

PLANNING FOR COLLEGE IN THE CAR SEAT YEARS

Rachelle Hernandez
Senior Vice Provost for Enrollment Management
University of Texas at Austin

Dear Parents,

Because I work in higher education—and, more than that, in college admissions—fellow parents often ask me for advice about college planning. I recall attending my oldest son's kindergarten welcome picnic, when another parent approached me and asked about the quality of our local high schools. As we chatted, it became clear that her ultimate question was which high school would best support her son's chances of getting into the college of his choice. She'd been thinking about this since her son was in preschool. I realized that my husband and I, too, had been thinking about and "planning for" college, though our focus was much different. We have three sons, none older than elementary school–age. Our youngest is three years old. We took the following steps when our older boys were small and have continued to use them as a guide for our youngest.

- *Attending the "right" school.* We had been thinking about high school choices since our oldest was a toddler. However, from the vantage point of my professional life, I have seen value in many different school options and choices. Certainly school resources help (and that's what many people look at first), but I frequently meet exceptional college students who come from under-resourced schools. I've learned from those experiences, in particular that parent engagement matters a lot. I've seen the impact and importance of parents who are connected to their child's school—whether through volunteering or simply staying up to date with school communications. A school's commitment to its students matters too. No matter the financial resources they may have, elementary and secondary schools that commit themselves to their students' development and success are key to positive and impactful college preparation. I've had too many conversations over the years that include the phrase, "But, our child attends the best high school . . ."

In the end, family engagement in a child's education makes the biggest difference. The elementary school our older sons attended wasn't highly resourced, but it had teachers invested in their students and a community of parents who were present in their children's lives and the operations of the school. We knew this was key for our children's educational foundation. It ultimately is our responsibility as parents to make sure our young children are engaged in school.

- *Money. Money. Money.* Because I work in college enrollment and my husband works in finance, you might think the college savings process would be easy for us. After all, I should have a clear understanding of the value of saving for college, and he should know the right financial tools and avenues to use to get us to a goal. But finding the right approach has not always been easy. We spent a great deal of time trying to figure out the right savings tools, what we should save, and how to save. After much consideration, we ultimately chose a conventional approach, a college savings plan. The plan provided us an opportunity to save what we could and the security of knowing that the money could be used for a variety of education options in the future. Our children could use the money for their undergraduate experience or for graduate school, or, if any was left over after all that, they could gift it to another family member. In the end, we learned a powerful lesson about the value of taking the time to research options and make the choice that was best for our needs and situation. "Keeping up with the Joneses" doesn't usually work. Doing what is best for your family always does.

Every little bit counts. As our children reached school age, we discovered that saving for their college years—a still-distant prospect—is much like any other major financial decision: if you wait until you have enough money, you will never have enough money. Finance professionals typically advise people to take care of their own retirement before they begin to save for their children's college education. We have tried to remain attentive to our retirement. But we also recognized very early that saving, even if just a little along the way, makes a big difference and sets us on a stronger path for the future.

I advise new working parents whose children have moved beyond daycare and into the primary grades not to simply celebrate their newfound income. Instead, carve out a percentage of what you would have paid for daycare and put it into your children's savings plan. Even a small portion of what you paid weekly for daycare will help and quickly accumulate. As our children aged out of daycare, my husband and I allocated resources as though we still had those expenses, only this time replacing the daycare expense with college savings. This was our way of caring for our children into their future.

In addition to what we do for our children, they also are required to put some of their gift money and allowance into their college fund. We have not made that optional. We are trying to teach them while they are still quite young that they too will be responsible for paying for some of their college expenses. We also want them to see the value of the payoff that comes from saving and investing in their future, a skill they will need to manage their finances during and after college. We hope it will help them understand that though we cannot give them everything they want, we will work with them to ensure that they have what they need. My middle son—a competitive child—now tracks his account to see what he is earning toward college. He has not yet amassed a lot of money, but he works hard to try to have the leading amount saved among his siblings. We are glad that at least one of our children seems to have learned this lesson!

- *Focus on the basics.* My longtime mentor used this phrase regularly and it has special meaning for parents as they guide their children through the school years. The development of two habits of the mind is particularly important when children are young: reading and personal responsibility.

Reading. If I could tell my younger self one key piece of advice that would prove especially valuable as a parent, it would be to focus on the importance of reading when your kids are young and to keep reading as they grow. I love to read. I have friends whose children love to read. So I had a hard time understanding why my son did not enjoy it. He has a highly creative mind, and he loves to be read to but does not like to read by himself. I have learned along the way that he is not the only child, and certainly not the only boy, who does not enjoy reading. As it turns out, he loves math. Still, we work at reading a little bit every day because I know that anything he chooses to do in life, even if math remains his focus, will require exceptional reading and language skills. The discipline he learns from establishing good reading habits also will strongly support his success in college.

Personal responsibility. My oldest son to me: "Mom, I thought I turned that assignment in. But, I scored in the ninety-eighth percentile on the math test. So it's fine. It's not like I don't understand it." Me to my oldest son: "Ugh."

I meet many students who are exceptionally bright, but whose grades do not reflect either their talent or their potential. These students often perform well on tests, but their grades do not reflect the personal discipline and commitment that will be required to succeed in college. The practice and discipline that come from completing homework is critically important to a student's success in college. I have a child who is a strong test taker. But we work on organization and submitting homework and taking care of personal responsibilities. Every day.

As a family, we have encouraged our children to embrace age-appropriate personal responsibility as a foundation step for building strong learning habits for a lifetime. As our older boys began elementary school, we focused on helping them to learn that their homework is their responsibility, letting them know that it matters as much as or more than the final grade they receive. I see far too many prospective and current college students who cram and test well but who simply are not adequately prepared for the rigors and independence of a college education. I know as a higher education professional that a student's daily performance in class demands work ethic and personal responsibility. As it turns out, strong work ethic and a well-developed sense of personal responsibility also are strong predictors of success in college. Our family has focused on developing personal responsibility not just with school, but with basic household responsibilities and outside activities, as well.

We are not perfect, but we try not to do for our children things that they can and should do for themselves. We began with simple chores, like putting things away when we were cleaning the house or following the calendar for important dates. Our middle son began helping with laundry when he was in early elementary school and by third grade had learned to do his own. I now have some comfort that wherever he goes to college, he will at least have clean socks and underwear! These are little things, but we see glimmers of the independence and personal responsibility our children will need to succeed in college and in life.

I have a favorite quote that speaks to me as a parent: "Behind every great kid is a mom who is pretty sure she's screwing it all up." We do the best we can as parents. I have learned from experience, both as a parent and as a college professional, to focus on the simple building blocks that provide the foundation for a life. As importantly, I've learned that comparing myself as a parent to other parents, or comparing my children to other children, is a recipe for disaster. Each of my kids is their own interesting self, and neither my husband nor I are the same parents as our friends. And that's just the way it should be. Countless conversations and encounters with students and families has taught me that although learning from others can be helpful, comparing usually isn't. Your child's personality and talents are unique to her or him. As parents, we must aim not to make perfect decisions—that isn't possible—but rather to make the best decisions we can each day for our children and their futures, not always knowing how it will turn out.

The best thing I can do for my children to prepare them for college is to be present in their lives now, when they are young, guiding them along the steps of their journey. We care that they learn, but we also care that they develop their interests and talents to become the well-rounded and interesting people we think they certainly will be. We hope to open their worlds to provide them with college opportunities we did not have, perhaps opportunities we cannot even imagine today. Ultimately, we seek to guide them to make choices that allow them to live meaningful lives, contributing to society and the common good as responsible people able to take care of themselves and others and make a difference in the lives of those who matter to them. That's a common wish among parents, but even if they achieve most of it, we won't have to worry about "screwing things up"!

THREE

Fit

My head knocks against the stars.
My feet are on the hilltops.
My finger-tips are in the valleys and shores of universal life.
Down in the sounding foam of primal things I reach my hands
    and play with pebbles of destiny.
—**Carl Sandburg, "Who Am I?"**

✉ **From Kristin R. Tichenor, Senior Vice President,**
Worcester Polytechnic Institute, Massachusetts

Dear Parents,

Our lives as parents are filled with a steady stream of stress points. As our children age, the stakes seem to get higher. Are they doing well in school? Are they making good choices about their friends? Are they healthy? Are they happy? The college selection process, in many ways, is the apex of this high-anxiety endeavor we call parenting. However involved you may be in your children's college selection process, keep in mind that it's your daughter or son heading off, not you. Yes, they will come home over breaks, but as students and young adults they will be laying the groundwork for life on their own. College is the point where our roads diverge. As a parent, you want to ensure as best you can that the school they attend will give them the tools they need to live happily ever after.

As parents, we have somewhat limited control over the college search and selection process. We surely can set parameters—distance from home, cost of attendance, and so forth—and we can set expectations. Timely graduation and gainful employment are perennial parental favorites. But ultimately, our children need to decide where to apply and where to enroll. For those of us accustomed to managing every aspect of our children's lives, turning over the reins can be incredibly stressful.

When my eldest child started looking at colleges a couple of years ago, I was determined to be a model parent. Yet, when she suggested visiting colleges in other parts of the country, I found myself rationalizing why long-distance options wouldn't work. I preferred that she attend a school closer to home. My husband immediately interrupted my thought process: "I thought you said that the most important thing is to find the right fit. Don't we want her to attend a school where she will thrive, regardless of location?" To turn my argument, he used my own words and advice, which I regularly share with students and parents as part of my job! And he was right; I had projected my own anxiety about my daughter leaving home onto her search.

Still, it got worse. We visited a dozen institutions, and she fell in love with the school she was least likely to get into. I routinely advise students to try to visit schools within reach from an admissions standpoint. To do otherwise inevitably increases the odds of an unhappy outcome. Having spent my entire professional career working in college admissions, I know how capricious decisions can be at highly selective schools. It is rarely about a student's capacity to succeed academically. The admission pools at selective colleges include more than enough academically qualified candidates. Rather, those schools work to create a balance of talent and student characteristics. From the moment my daughter submitted her application to that selective college, I became a nervous wreck, sharing my angst daily with colleagues, who reacted with a combination of bemusement and patience. I ultimately learned that this becomes the point where a parent needs to keep her anxiety to herself!

In the end, I took away an important lesson: our job as parents is to help our sons and daughters maintain a sense of perspective, even if that is sometimes difficult for us. The goal is to provide them with a good education that allows them to pursue the career or passion of their choice. That can happen at any number of schools, regardless of mascot or bumper sticker. That is the secret to the happy ending, for them and for you!

P.S. She got in!

✉ **From Brian Lindeman, Director of Financial Aid, Macalester College, Minnesota**

Dear Parents,

I recall my own college preparation as a series of hoops through which I was instructed to jump. In high school, I took the "right" classes, earned good grades, and did relatively well on standardized tests. In theory, I was well prepared for college work. But the hoop I hadn't yet jumped through was, in retrospect, the most important one: developing a true passion for learning and a sense of accountability for my own intellectual progress.

I am the father of two sons, a ninth grader and a seventh grader. My greatest hope for their academic and college preparation is that each will develop their own genuine academic passions. I am much less concerned about which college they are admitted to than whether they truly enjoy learning. I'm lucky that my children attend a wonderful school with excellent teachers. I have no doubt they will be academically prepared for college work. But as a parent, I see my role as helping my boys connect what they learn in school to the world around them. Joy in learning, as well as critical thinking skills, comes from seeing how most issues are multidimensional. I want to take advantage of the opportunities I have as a parent to demonstrate that to my kids, whether through a political discussion at the dinner table or by watching a television documentary together. Because they are teenage boys, they are not always interested in sharing their thoughts and opinions with their parents, but it's absolutely worth it to try to get them to talk! I feel sure that building these skills—discussing controversial issues, listening to different perspectives, appreciating healthy debate—will help them take advantage of their future college experience as they develop their own perspectives.

I have a similar view when it comes to extracurricular activities:

I hope for engagement and dedication to things that really excite and interest them. My kids happen to be very athletic—a genetic quirk that puzzles their decidedly nonathletic parents—and I sometimes catch myself wishing that they'd branch out into drama, speech, music, robotics, or Rubik's Cube. But the reality is that their passions are found on the field, the court, and the track; they love competition and are dedicated to their teams. This passion is what we should hope for and value as parents, rather than a laundry list of activities in which our children are less deeply engaged but that we think will "look good" on a college application. I'll hope and expect that they try some new things as they age, but I'm also deeply pleased that they have found activities outside of school that they love and to which they are willing to commit time and effort.

It's their journey, not ours. As parents, we should always keep that in mind. We can (and should) guide, cajole, and even nag occasionally. We should challenge them to think harder and do their best work, and we should remember that college is not the ultimate goal—it is only the very beginning of their lives as adults. And we should not forget to enjoy them while we have the privilege of witnessing their progress and their successes.

 From Eric Staab, Dean of Admission and Financial Aid, Kalamazoo College, Michigan

Dear Parents,

As you begin your college search, know that you may encounter a well-meaning aunt, uncle, or family friend who will eagerly deliver their expert college-search advice to your child. Those discussions typically start with the question, "So what do you want to study?" Unfortunately, that query is akin to an annoying job interview question, "Where do you see yourself ten years from now?" Rarely is the answer grounded in reality. People usually tailor it to the expectations of the person asking the question.

So why ask the question at all? In the case of looking for a college, is your daughter or son's current academic interest the best variable for deciding where to attend college? Often, no.

As I toured several college campuses with my son, I watched his answer to "What do you want to study" change from Spanish, to physics, and then to computer science. He wanted to study all of them, basing his interest on experiences he had had in high school courses. A significant percentage of college students will change their major at least once during the course of their undergraduate years. This shouldn't come as a surprise given that they will be exposed to many new ideas and areas of study once enrolled. True, there are unicorns in the woods that know exactly what they want to be when they grow up, but sightings of these rare beasts are uncommon. Resist the idea of guiding your children to the college that has "the right" academic program. Look for a school that will stretch them academically and will give them the tools to be critical and creative thinkers. At the same time, though, take care not to assume that either you or your child knows today what they will become tomorrow.

My son has now completed his first year of college and has taken classes in all of the subjects he identified as potential majors during his college search. He still doesn't know what he will declare as his major in his sophomore year, but he consistently has taken interesting, varied, and challenging courses, which collectively will shape who he becomes. More power to him!

It's about You

It is an extraordinary privilege to spend a career working on a college campus. Colleges typically teem with life and activity—they exude the passion and energy of youth and the dreams of the future. At the most basic level, the college experience lives at the intersection of aspiration and opportunity, which is why many of us have chosen to dedicate our lives to working in higher education. Though it doesn't always come through in our promotional material, colleges and universities, and our admissions offices in particular, fully understand the importance of choosing wisely and seeking a good fit. It is in our best interests as institutions to ensure that our schools also meet and serve the best interests of our students. Anything else reduces the admission process to little more than a numbers game. Our primary ambition is—or ought to be—to enroll students who can and will take full advantage of the experiences we provide.

Choose wisely. And choose for you, not for someone else. Too many students and their parents begin the college search process wondering which school will accept them. Can I get into this college? Am I good enough for this school or kind of school? That's the wrong way to start and end. Instead, it is far more productive to construct the experience from the opposite angle. "What kind of college experience do I want? Which college is right for me and why? Which places represent the best fit and offer the best experience in relation to my goals and ambitions?" It's akin to flipping the question, "Am I right for this college?" to "Is this college right for me?" The approach works as well for consideration of highly selective colleges as it does for less-selective or even open-access institutions. Fit ultimately addresses the question about match, and match is a two-way street—a match that works for both the student and the college.

Importantly, avoid the temptation to seek enrollment at a particular college or university because either you or your son or daughter feels deserving of it or entitled to it. In fact, that approach (which admission professionals at selective colleges see frequently) nearly always provides a poor frame for college decision making. It gives away responsibility for an active consideration of fit. As often as not, it can set up disappointment instead of joy—in the form of either a rejected application or an experience that does not rise to its imagined level.

So rather than seeking an institution based on some kind of assumed entitlement, at the point of both college consideration and selection, students and parents should take the time to explore their values and ambitions, own their choice, and have more than a passing understanding of why they think a particular experience will work well for them.

Beyond the Guidebook

Years ago, when I first started working at the College of Saint Benedict and Saint John's University, our then library director told me that we were home to the eleventh-largest library collection among all liberal arts colleges in the country, a group that included more than two hundred colleges. I was impressed. Having spent a lot of time in the library as an undergraduate student, I believe that libraries powerfully represent a school's commitment to knowledge and learning. On further reflection after learning about our library, I wondered what the raw statistic—presented to me then as a kind of feature or merit badge—really meant. What if, in a digital age, libraries had become little more than mausoleums for books and journals? What do our students learn as a result of having access to our extensive collection? The statistic alone had a kind of wink-and-nod quality to it, presuming the hearer would fully understand or even simply assume its meaning and value. Unfortunately, that's a too-common approach for presenting data and facts on colleges and universities.

I have vivid memories as a high school senior several decades ago of perusing *Peterson's Guide to Colleges and Universities*, presented in microscopically small print, looking for information about various schools. Although print publications remain, today the Internet provides the quickest access to guidebook-style resources intended to help students and their families learn about and parse the vast collegiate landscape in America. These resources come with solution-oriented banner headlines: "Find Your Perfect College" (Unigo), "Your College Search Starts Here" (Fiske Interactive Online College Search), and "Your College Decision Headquarters" (Cappex), among many others.

College guides provide a handy and useful resource for kicking off and defining a student's college search. They typically present pages of statistics otherwise not easily accessed, often with options to compare data among schools. They almost always focus on how much or how

LOOKING BEYOND THE GUIDEBOOK

As you participate in your child's college search, I encourage you to look beyond the guidebook and the numeric summaries they provide. Prepare a list of questions about the college experience that you can ask of any school your son or daughter considers. You should expect colleges to provide evidence for each of their answers.

- What learning skills does this college best impart?

- How do students here develop as people? How does this experience contribute to key life skills, like self-confidence, independent learning, and leadership?

- Describe the academic environment at this college. How do current students describe their academic experience and its quality? How do they describe their own academic commitment? How do students describe their relationship with faculty or other students? How do they describe and evaluate the academic experiences the college offers?

- How does the college support its students' success, from first enrollment through graduation? What percentage of students persist from year to year? What percent graduate, and how long does it take them to graduate?

- Describe the social environment at this college. How do current students describe relationships with other students? How do they describe the campus community?

- What are the employment or graduate school outcomes and experiences of the school's young graduates? What do they do and how do they describe their work?

- How well are the school's graduates prepared for their professional lives and careers? How do they describe the value of their undergraduate experience to their postcollege experiences and aspirations? Would they choose the college again if they could start over?

many of something, reporting total enrollment, racial and ethnic composition of the student body, price of attendance, student-to-faculty ratios, typical SAT scores, spending per student, retention or graduation rates, average class size, or even the size of the library collection.

Colleges themselves provide similar information on their own websites. The data generally are easy to compile and count and provided in small bites (nowadays minus the bifocal-inducing print size). Collectively, they paint a broad-brush picture of the body of a school and its features.

However, even though guidebook resources can quickly and easily provide reams of data about a school, the information typically (though not always) is provided without any special context. Students and parents often must assign their own meaning to the data, sometimes being left to conclude that more of some things must be better—like spending per student—while less of other things must be better—like students per faculty member. Unfortunately, data never speak well for themselves.

Listening to a panel of undergraduate students describe their experiences in the college admission process, one young woman said wistfully that she wished she had known more about relationships among students than statistics about students—because it was the relationships, not the data, that shaped her experience. A wise insight. College guides rarely provide insights into a school's soul, purpose, experience, or value. What kinds of experiences do the college's students have and how do they describe the value of those experiences? How do students report having changed by the end of their college experience? What kinds of value do their alumni cite for having attended the college? What learning or social experiences contributed most (or least) to their life after college? That information typically is difficult and costly for colleges to gather and count, but it provides much more insight into what a prospective student might actually experience than is conveyed by a ratio, a test score, an enrollment statistic, or a dollar figure.

Rankings, Rankings Everywhere

A long time ago, I asked a college president I knew well what he thought of his institution's placement on the annual *U.S. News and World Report*'s ranking of colleges and universities. He said he never thought about it. I didn't believe it.

We live in a culture that loves ranked lists. We rate everything from cars, toasters, and fruit drinks to hospitals, attorneys, and colleges. Rankings appeal to our fascination with finishing first and being branded a winner. This is hardly a new phenomenon. The first issue of *Consumer's Union Reports* (the predecessor to today's *Consumer Reports*) appeared in 1936 and included reviews of milk, cereal, and soap. The publication still rates cereals and soap and at least some kinds of milk. The first edition of the *Guinness Book of World Records* was published in 1955 and became an immediate bestseller. People still compete to land on its lists of achievement. The 1977 *Book of Lists* was a bestseller through multiple reprints and editions for more than a decade.

Colleges and universities like lists too. Many look to the August to October period, when many annual rankings are released, with a sense of triumph, fear, or foreboding, sometimes all three. Mostly, we like appearing on top of lists, at least the good lists. Rankings and lists often validate our sense of self. At other times, depending on where we land, they offend it. *U.S. News and World Report* published its first "America's Best Colleges" ranking in 1983. If readership numbers are an indicator of interest and success, it was a brilliant idea, though I suspect colleges, not students or parents, make up a significant portion of the readership. The success of the *U.S. News* rankings has spawned an industry of "me too" guides, including *Forbes, Money, Time, Newsweek, Kiplinger's,* and *Princeton Review,* among others. Almost every facet of college life now appears somewhere on a ranked list, from schools with the best food to best surfing schools and even "most Beyoncé" colleges. Beyond the commercial lists, state and federal governments also have gotten into the game, producing a variety of lists and tools that purport to provide consumers information in support of good college decision making. Each list, commercial or government, tries to capture someone's attention. Unfortunately, almost none measures or values exactly the same thing, leaving students and parents with more information but less comprehensive knowledge than ever.

Colleges willingly provide huge amounts of data to guidebook producers each year, thus ensuring the future of ranked lists. Those lists seem to convey information objectively (though the data underlying them are gathered in wildly different and often poorly understood ways) and feature data readily counted and measured. They distill sometimes-complicated information for easy consumption, satisfying our human need for order and simplicity. The age of rankings has arisen in no small part because of higher education's inability to collect and convey compelling, comparative, and easily understood information on its own. Plus, we like winners and want to associate ourselves with winning organizations—and rankings clearly identify winners.

Rankings imply not only best or good, but also, by extension, worst or bad. Over many years, I've often been asked the seemingly simple question, "Is that a *good* school or a *bad* school?" My own children asked it often when they were young—usually after watching a football bowl game—but even later as they engaged in their own college search. I dislike the question because it's most often based on little more than a fleeting brand impression, a singular and limited experience or, worst of all, hearsay. But it does raise an interesting point: Are colleges objectively good or bad? I don't think rankings and statistics provide the answer. Those almost always favor highly resourced institutions, the assumption being that more resources always equals better. And that may or may not be true.

Ultimately, it's not about the level of resources an institution has at its disposal but rather what it does with those resources, despite how much or how little it has, to make a difference in the lives of the students it serves. An under-resourced college, for example, may not have the financial wherewithal to do everything it would like to do, but it may serve its students and its mission well with the resources it has available. In other words, success ought not be measured by dollars spent or how much of this or that but rather by how effectively those dollars and resources are used in support of student learning. Accreditation, a process that degree-granting colleges and universities of all types, sizes, and pedigree must go through periodically, is designed to ensure that schools meet standards of performance consistent with their mission and their claims of value, at any resource level. It's a quality assurance process designed to protect and advance the interests of students. Though some colleges and universities may perform better or worse than others in relation to any number of criteria, I don't subscribe to the idea that a college should be subject to either the broadly dismissive or starry-eyed conclusion that it is objectively bad or good. Good or bad, like beauty, is in the eyes of the beholder. The appropriate question, then, is not whether an institution is good or bad, but rather does it perform well in relation to my needs, expectations, and aspirations.

So what should parents make of rankings, best-of lists, and consideration of good and bad? First, understand that rankings and perceptions of good or bad mean different things at different times to different students. For all of the attention that rankings often receive in the media and on college campuses, relatively few students find them persuasive at the point they make their decision. In fall 2016, fewer than one in five first-time new entering students at all four-year colleges and universities nationally cited rankings in national magazines as "very important" to their final college selection.[1] They matter most to students enrolled at highly selective private or public universities, but even then, fewer than four in ten students newly enrolled at those institutions describe them as "very useful."

Most often, ranked lists anchor their standard for "best" across only a limited number of criteria, typically a mix of "how much" or "how many" data gathered from colleges in combination with data on perceived quality collected in surveys. Most rankings give preference to schools with more resources, rewarding wealth as a proxy for quality. More importantly, they value being first over everything else, essentially endorsing the idea that you don't win gold, you lose silver.[2] The perils for individual colleges become immediately clear. The most effective way for any single institution to rise in a group of ranked institutions is to seek to perform the same as or better than the institutions positioned ahead of it. The point is not to be different, or even generally better, but only better in relation to a limited handful of fixed criteria. Unfortunately, that approach does little to effectively serve the vast array of students seeking to enroll in colleges and universities across the country. American higher education is not characterized by the small number of institutions that rise to the top of lists but rather by its diversity and its ability to meet the needs of students of all types, abilities, and levels.

Are Harvard, Princeton, Amherst, or Williams the best colleges in the country? (They are, according to some rankings.) For some students, the answer undoubtedly is yes, but for others—including many very good students—it is no. As you approach rankings and develop your framework of "best," think carefully about what they measure and what you value. Rankings can be helpful on the front end of a college search process to help you sort out choice "neighborhoods"—offering a tool to help identify and examine institutions of similar mission, scale, and brand reputation. However, because a one-size-fits-all criterion fits neither all institutions nor all students, the utility of rankings decreases as you work more deeply into your college search. They do not and cannot describe the experiences your son or daughter will have or need. "Caveat emptor": buyer beware.

Fit, Not Features

If you have not visited a college campus in some time, or have never had that experience, prepare to have your senses jolted. The days of the ascetic collegiate experience—often defined by austere living spaces, drab food, and highly regulated and limited lifestyle choices—have long passed. From academic and social opportunities to creature comforts, colleges of all types today offer a remarkable range of experiences and amenities. Colleges work very hard to put their best foot forward as they present themselves to students and families. Campuses now routinely feature comfortable residential facilities, lovely manicured grounds, state-of-the-art athletic and recreational centers, highly sophisticated classroom and laboratory technology, and vast and varied experiential learning opportunities. Even college food, the last bastion of a dreary institutional stereotype, has gone upscale, as campus dining halls now routinely provide eating choices unimaginable—or simply unimagined—in days gone by. I have visited many campuses over many years, and I continue to experience a sense of wonder on every visit. Contrary to images that cast higher education as wedded to an ancient past, colleges are places of continuous change, invention, and reinvention. It is difficult to walk on to a college campus these days and not come away amazed by the sheer range of options, opportunities, and amenities offered. We care about making a strong impression. Features—particularly those that students can see and touch or easily understand—cast a powerful glow. We want prospective students and their parents to fall in love with us.

But alluring and impressive as they may be, features have limits. My family visited a college with one of our high school sons and spent most of our tour viewing residence halls, dining halls, and campus greenways. The campus was beautiful and impressive, but we learned little from our guide about what the college actually did or what it valued. Those parts of the college experience received scant attention on the tour. My son was agog, lost in love in the sea of attractive images. I was aghast.

The term *commodity* typically is used in a consumer context to describe products like bread or toothpaste—ubiquitous, mass-produced necessities that, in spite of the seeming number of choices and the power of advertising to create preferences and apparent differences, are nearly indistinguishable from each other. Most people who work in higher education would resist as both distasteful and inappropriate the notion that a college education is similar to a consumer commodity. We profess to understand the significance of what we do from the ground level and assert a refined and meaningful sense of the distinctive value we provide at our individual institutions. We do not see sameness or mass production.

And yet, our assertions notwithstanding, we colleges often find ourselves in a self-made commodity trap. As higher education has expanded and become more expansive, reaching more people with more programs than ever, it has become less discretely distinguishable, particularly as institutions of all types use similar language and images to describe who they are and what they do. On the whole, we most often look and act more alike than unalike.

As my children have gone through their college search processes, I have been struck by the sameness of the early mail coming to our home: nearly identical letters making nearly identical claims and offering nearly identical "rewards" for returning an enclosed mailer (sort of like Cracker Jack rewards, only this time more like handy 1-2-3 guides on how to select a college). Oftentimes different colleges use the same mail house to process their rewards. Not much in those early pitch pieces sets one college apart from the other, a particular complication when more than one search piece arrives on the same day. If we had looked only at those mailed materials, we could have reasonably concluded that nearly all colleges are friendly, caring learning communities dedicated to academic excellence and the development of the whole person.

Even the academic programs offered by colleges and universities, considered across all institutions, often project sameness. A quick perusal of the more than twenty-seven hundred institutions offering bachelor's degrees that are included in the online *Peterson's* guide indicates that nearly seventeen hundred offer degrees in psychology, more than fifteen hundred in biology or history, and nearly twelve hundred in economics, just to name a few.[3] Any individual school must understand the distinctiveness of its own academic programs and its own faculty, but it has not been my experience that the typical prospective college student and parents are either so well informed or so discerning. What we understand on campus as differentiation or specialization at our own school is not nearly as clear among prospective students as they consider many institutions at the same time. We see distinction; they see thousands of similarly described psychology, biology, history, or economics programs, which can make it difficult for prospective students

---

DEFINING FIT: WHO AM I?

I encourage you to ask your children to complete the following four sentences as they begin their college search (and certainly before they complete their college applications or consider institutional features). You can complete them too, as a way to frame a family conversation later. There are no right or wrong answers; it isn't a test and no grade is awarded. Rather, each sentence provides a tool for self-understanding and an opportunity for reflection. Completing each sentence will go a long way toward helping you and your children discern a good college match.

I am . . . What makes me tick? What kinds of activities or experiences motivate, interest, or excite me? What makes me comfortable? What makes me uncomfortable?

I expect . . . What do I expect of my collegiate experience as a student? What do I expect my collegiate experience to provide me? What do I expect of myself in college?

I value . . . What values do I hold most dear (values that are nonnegotiable)? What kinds of experiences do I value?

I need . . . What kinds of community or services or support will I need as a student? What do I need a college to do for me?

Be honest and realistic as you complete each sentence. Avoid the temptation to add "I want," because wants inevitably yield wish lists. When you or your daughter or son has completed each sentence, keep them handy when considering and applying to schools. Use your responses—which reflect what is most important to you and about you—as a way to evaluate features, values, and experiences at the colleges you consider.

or their parents to meaningfully or more than superficially distinguish differences and, more importantly, advantages. No matter how well packaged, features typically do not define the beating heart of a college or university. You will need to dig deeper than guidebooks and mass mailings to find real differentiation and value.

But before you consider or discern the collegiate features you find most interesting or valuable, start with fit: "What defines who I am and what I value and need? How does that match or fit with the schools I am considering?" Ultimately, at the point of choosing, your daughter or son will need more than a superficial understanding of why any single school represents a good match with their preparation, expectations, personal values, characteristics, and aspiration. Absent a clear understanding of self and fit, all of the features will look good, like shiny objects. And you will be unable to meaningfully tell one shiny object from the other.

Beats versus Bose

During his senior year in high school, my oldest son's over-ear headphones broke. In the world of a 17-year-old (and a 17-year-old athlete, fond of the smooth look headphones cast when entering a gym), this represented something of a catastrophe requiring an immediate remedy. Predictably, he first turned to his mother and me and asked if we would buy him new headphones—a euphemistic request for a blank check. Predictably, at least to his mother and me, though less so to him, the answer was no. This was a real opportunity for a teaching moment. We reminded him that he was working at the time and had the resources to purchase his own headphones. So losing out on the free option, he began a research process that rivaled a major academic project. Because the purchase now required his own resources, the question of value moved to the forefront. The selection ultimately came down to headphones by Beats and Bose. Each featured exceptional sound, though the Beats clearly represented the "cool" choice. Beats by Dre. Beats by Apple. A personal statement in the making. Though these two final choices offered nearly identical sound specifications, the Beats cost twice as much as the Bose. He had to make a choice. Were the Beats, differentiated principally by their social value, worth $150 more than the Bose? He reflected on the value question for what seemed to me a long time. In the end, he chose the Bose headphones. Though he had the resources to buy the Beats, he ultimately did not think they were worth the extra money—money he could put to other, better uses. So went a small but meaningful lesson in defining value.

As consumers, we consider comparative value and worth all the time, with nearly every purchase we make. For most products, experiences, or services there is no such thing as absolute value. We typically understand the value of one thing only in relation to something else. Is this thing worth the price in relation to that thing? Beats or Bose? The simple economic equation goes like this: when considering a purchase among several competing items, the incremental value of the more costly product or experience must be greater than the incremental effort (financial, psychic, or social) required to obtain it. The academic language notwithstanding, it is the simplest equation of consumer economics. It also is immutable. It captures the way we buy things. What value advantage makes something worth purchasing, even at the price of extraordinary effort? Marketing seeks to influence the choice and persuade us, but the decision of worth and value ultimately rests with us as consumers.

It's easy to imagine purchasing a college education in the very same way. We can compare institutions on any number of characteristics or promises and then choose the one that best meets some overall standard of value, that neither requires nor presumes choosing the less or least expensive option. National research on how families pay for college clearly indicates that families are willing to commit significant financial resources in support of what they believe to be their best choice. A 2017 survey by student loan giant Sallie Mae indicated that nearly nine in ten college students and their parents were willing to stretch themselves financially to obtain the education they deemed best for their future.[4]

Value reflects more than price. It demands an answer to the question: "Is this school worth the investment of my financial resources, as well as time and effort?" An understanding of value also does not presume the ideal. That is, if price or admission standards or geography were no object, for example, where would you choose to enroll? But standards and geography and other issues are very real and often act as constraints on choices, forcing families to balance "what I want to do" (the ideal) with "what I can do" (the real). As parents, we can guide those conversations, helping our children (as well as ourselves) sort out what value and worth really mean.

As my oldest son approached D-Day for making his college choice, he wrestled with how to decide. I had asked him to prepare formal lists identifying pros and cons of the schools he considered in relation to his expectations and values. Unfortunately, he did not complete that assignment (a clear indication that my advice was interpreted through the prism of "dad" rather than "enrollment professional"!), which left him a bit adrift about how to bring the process to closure. In the end, he wrestled with two choices, both schools that matched his interests and aspirations very well. In many ways, the schools were similar, but the incremental difference in net price was substantial: one school would have cost our family well over $100,000 more over four years than the other. Rather than simply use the price difference as a way to force a choice, my wife and I instead asked him, "Could you tell us why you think this school is worth that much more than the other?" It was, perhaps, an unfair question, expecting an 18-year-old to have a deep comparative understanding of two colleges. Most colleges themselves struggle to articulate how or why they are different from their peers and competitors. I knew he would struggle with an answer. In the end, he chose the smaller price tag not because it cost less but rather because he could not (nor could I) define enough difference or value to warrant paying the higher price. Had the two finalists been different, where the value of the one clearly exceeded the value of the other, he perhaps would have made a different choice. He learned, as did I, that value is relative.

As with fit, value requires a realistic assessment of self. Choosing a college is a big decision for both kids and parents—financially, developmentally, socially, and academically. Though students today typically apply for admission at many schools, in the end the decision most often comes down to just two choices. At that point, you will need some way of making the choice, discerning one college from the other. It can be difficult, particularly because the finalists may appear quite similar (which explains how they reached the finalist stage). It's best to have an understanding of value from the beginning, one that allows you to reasonably weigh and consider competing choices. Beginning with some sense of the end in mind will save a lot of angst later.

More Than a Major

Students and parents often think of fit and school choice in terms of academic major: Does the school offer a particular program of interest? It's a common way to choose a college, or at least a way to narrow a college search. But, caveat emptor. Several years ago, a friend and long-time enrollment professional said to me, "Every spring as the admission deadline approaches, I wake up in the middle of the night in a cold sweat thinking that my family eats because of the choices of 18-year-old boys and girls." A keen insight born of experience. Choices and preferences change as our children are exposed to new people, new ideas, and new ways of thinking.

"What do you want to major in?" Nearly all parents ask it of their preparing-to-head-to-college children, as do aunts, uncles, family friends, and anyone else trying to engage with teenagers in a conversation about education. Given the frequency of the question, it should come as no surprise that the vast majority of new students oblige and come to college having identified a likely college field of study (even though students attending four-year colleges do not have to formally choose a major until the end of their sophomore year). In the fall of 2016, 91 percent of all first-time new entering students at four-year colleges and universities nationally identified a likely academic major; fewer than one in ten described themselves as undecided about a major.[5] It's not a new phenomenon, and students today actually are more likely to describe themselves as undecided about a major than they were in 1970, when 98 percent of new students identified a likely field of study.

On the one hand, students' confidence about both their interests and their future is admirable, suggesting a clearly thought-out direction. And it is a comfortable thought for most parents: make a plan and stick to it. "Undecided" suggests drift and clouded thinking. It also raises fears about time to completion. "Will my child spend the next decade in college trying to figure it out?" Reality, though, often plays out differently.

At my institutions, nearly 90 percent of new students each fall describe "a particular academic major that interests me" as important to their final college choice. Ultimately, though, six in ten of them will major in something different than what they expressed as likely when they arrived. Nearly all students still will complete their bachelor's degree within four years, and more than seven in ten will indicate that they would choose the same major again if they could start over, all in spite of doing something different than they originally imagined for themselves. Nationally, most students major in something different from that which they declared when they entered. As many as three-quarters of all college students nationally change their major during their undergraduate years, and the decision to switch may have little impact on time to completion.[6] First declaration of interest often is not a final declaration of interest, and parents should keep that in mind, as well as an open mind, as they navigate the admission process and examine schools with their sons and daughters.

Two stories stand out for me, one happy and the other not, about the pressure and peril of early interest in particular academic disciplines. Years ago, while speaking to a class about how our students make their major choices and the frequency with which they change their minds as undergraduates, a young woman revealed in a somber tone that she had wanted to major in philosophy, but her parents had insisted she major in a business management discipline (which they viewed as practical). She had no interest in majoring in business but yielded to her parents' expectations nonetheless. I still find her story haunting, in large part because of the clear sense of loss and sadness in her voice. I often have wondered in the years since if she ever had the courage to speak to her parents about her real interests, and if they listened.

It can work the other way too. I had a student intern, Raj, a music major who was interested in working in my office to develop his re-search skills. Raj arrived at college as a new student intending to become a physician—until he took his first physics course. He realized then that medicine and the sciences likely were not in his future. Music was not a random choice. He had participated in band and choir grow-ing up and had entered college as an accomplished vocal performer. More importantly, he loved music and was able to leverage its order and structure to develop deep skills that could serve a wide variety of professional pursuits. His parents supported his choice, and today he is a successful fund-raising professional, a job that requires and values math skills, strong communication, public performance, and team-work, as well as a deep understanding of audience, all skills he learned and honed as a music major.

With the notable exceptions of specialized professional fields like engineering, accounting, nursing, or teaching, the names of academic disciplines or departments often say little about the broad skills developed by studying them. This is why direct pathways linking academic majors to professional occupations are at best difficult, and sometimes impossible, to reasonably define. Few academic majors prepare students for a singular profession or occupation. Well-constructed and delivered, most instead should provide students with a variety of skills to succeed in many different professions and occupations.

Some students really do know as 18-year-olds what they plan to do and be—and they make their college plans and choices accordingly. But coming out of high school, most have only a hazy understanding of their future or where their deepest interests, skills, and passions lie. With three of my four children still in secondary school, I often have to resist the temptation to ask them what they intend to study as college students or, worse, to impose my own thinking about what they should choose as majors. Instead, I try (mostly successfully) to stick with simple advice: major in something you enjoy. Learn as many skills and accumulate as many experiences as you can as a college student. And take care not to pick a college solely on the basis of what interests you at age 17 or 18. Your interests may change, and even if they don't, you will. Provide yourself the space and luxury to try new experiences and learn more about yourself and your world. Most of all, own your choice. It's yours to make, not mine.

Advising and encouraging uncertainty or indecision can be a scary path for parents. But a good college education should be less about linear certainty—do this, then that will follow—and more about an exploration of interests, experiences, and values. When I talk to groups of parents of prospective students during visits to campus, I always ask how many of them were certain about their future at age 18, and how many of them subsequently had followed the path they had in mind then. No one ever raises their hand. I know I couldn't. As you identify and visit colleges with your daughter or son, it's wise to ask fewer questions about academic majors and more about how the school advises and guides students to make and own their academic choices. A school should be able to articulate how it helps its students shape their choices and prepare them for lasting success after college. And that will make all the difference in the world.

FOUR

Money Matters

Money is only a tool. It will take you wherever you wish,
but it will not replace you as the driver.
—**Ayn Rand**

✉ **From Phil Trout, College Counselor, Minnetonka High School, Minnesota, and past president of the National Association for College Admission Counseling**

Dear Parents,

It almost always happens on a Monday. A student comes to see me in my office and announces, "Good morning, Mr. Trout. I need a scholarship!" I already know what happened the past weekend. The student has spent time talking with her or his parents about college—focusing in particular on the cost of attending college. The family has settled upon a certain dollar amount that they are prepared to spend. If a college costs more than that amount, parents often direct their children to seek scholarships—or to take out loans. If only I had a drawer I could open and pull out the cash!

Over several decades I have worked with thousands of students and their families. I often find myself explaining the difference be-tween merit-based aid and need-based aid. Frequently, I need to define what "scholarship" and "financial aid" mean. There are important differences, but the common message can be very encouraging to students and to their families: many students qualify for financial assistance to help make college more affordable.

But it isn't quite that easy. Students need to spend as much time thinking about—and researching—how they will pay for college as they already spend thinking about getting in.

I have always been amazed at the number of families who, as they go through their college search, have not completed a financial aid application but have questions and concerns about how they will find the resources to pay for college. Filing the FAFSA (the Free Application for Federal Student Aid) is an absolutely necessary step in the process. I encourage nearly every family to do it, particularly if they have any questions at all about their ability to pay for their child's college. I also recommend that parents take advantage of the many research tools readily available to them, including:

1. Checking out the net price calculator on every college's financial aid website.

2. Reading the average financial aid award and net price tuition reports available on the US Department of Education's College Navigator website (nces.ed.gov/collegenavigator).

3. Comparing the college scorecard for each institution on the student's college list (collegescorecard.ed.gov). The scorecard is an online tool prepared by the Department of Education to compare the cost and value of colleges and universities in the United States.

4. Contacting the financial aid office of any college to ask them specific questions about financial aid and paying for college.

All of this takes time, but it is time well spent by both the student and the family. And don't forget to visit your school's counseling office. We stand ready to help you!

From Robert Piechota, Director of Financial Aid, Saint John's University, Minnesota

Dear Parents,

Bewilderment and fear. I frequently spot those two emotions in parents facing the financial aid application process and the college affordability conversation with their kids. Unfortunately, those emotions often are just as quickly replaced by shock and despair when they receive their expected family contribution, the amount they are judged able to pay for college based on their federal financial aid application (the FAFSA). "Is that for just one year?" I get the job of bearing what mostly is challenging news: "Yes, that is right."

I have worked in financial aid for more than twenty-five years. Explaining an expected contribution and helping families to understand it comes with the territory. It hit home when my family had its own "Can that be right?" FAFSA moment. Our three children hit their college-age years over an eight-year period. We often had two in college at the same time and experienced the same shock as other parents after submitting our FAFSA. I bravely did not let my concern show too much but thought to myself, "How are we going to do this?"

What I soon realized, as many others have, is that my wife and I had not saved enough for our children's college costs. How much is enough? That's a difficult question to answer, but having something is always better than having nothing. For my kids, our insufficient savings meant that they would need to take out both federal and private loans, and my wife and I would tap a federal loan program for parents. As our children were growing up, we had had the best intentions to set aside funds for college. We knew it was on the horizon. But as often is the case, life derailed the best intentions: a period of unemployment for my wife reduced our ability to set aside funds for college, and getting back on track proved difficult. When our children reached the point of actually going to college, the full effect of it all became clear.

I sat down with my oldest to explain the options after she received financial aid offers from the colleges to which she had applied. The bottom line was simple: the college costs we would face and the amount of debt she could expect would vary based on the college she chose. As a financial aid professional, I was well aware of the available loan options and had a good working knowledge of the debt she could accumulate and reasonably afford to repay after she graduated. Still the conversation was difficult. The talk I had with my daughter and the choices she made ultimately altered the decisions my two other children made about which school to attend and how much they would be willing to borrow. These kinds of stories are common around kitchen tables and in financial aid offices.

I advise parents to talk with their children early—before beginning their college search—about college and the cost of higher education, including the cost of borrowing. Explore a variety of postsecondary options with your daughters and sons. Visit schools and ask questions about how they award their need-based and scholarship-based financial aid. Your expected contribution might not reflect what you believe is a realistic estimate of what you truly can contribute toward college. If so, you will need to explore other funding options and perhaps other college options, utilize college savings plans, and pursue scholarships. In many cases, even after all of that, student and parents still will need to borrow to finance college.

Given that the price of college continues to rise faster than income for many people, families need to prepare for their FAFSA moment and know their options well in advance. Be realistic about your finances and your college choices. Take the time to explore your financing options. Seemingly simple advice, but it can help manage stress and anxiety later in the process, when money conversations get much more difficult.

✉ **From Thomas F. Nelson Laird, Associate Professor, Higher Education and Student Affairs Director, Center for Postsecondary Research, Indiana University, Indiana**

Dear Parents,

I was given three important gifts as a kid by my parents, both of whom are liberal arts college graduates and have advanced degrees and careers related to higher education. The first was an unwavering belief in the power of a college education to better oneself and to open up worlds of opportunities. The second was a sense of responsibility. My parents viewed it as their job to pay for my sister's and my under-graduate educations. I was off the hook for my own education, but very much on the hook for my future children—that was clear! The third gift was closely linked to the second. Even though my parents took on the responsibility to pay for my college, they still imparted important knowledge about college financing—about the forms, key terms and concepts, and all of the different types of financial aid available.

As my wife and I started a family, we agreed that we would try to give these same three gifts to any children we had—we ended up with two daughters. For us, imparting these gifts meant starting to save when our first daughter was born and continuing to contribute to the savings account every month. Both of our daughters have college savings plans (that is, 529 plans), one each in Indiana (where we live) and in Minnesota (where our parents live and can contribute). It means talking to our children about the value of college and about how paying for college takes planning. It also means sharing our un-derstanding of how college financing works—that paying for college will likely include some combination of money from the family, loans, grants from the state and federal government, scholarships from the institution or other sources, and possibly some work-study (student employment) while in college (one way our children can contribute)—and seeking out guidance from knowledgeable others like high school counselors.

Our oldest daughter is 16 and starting the college search process. She still has a lot of learning to do over the next few years. As college costs continue to rise, my wife and I recognize that what we have saved is only a start. We will almost certainly take on debt as a part of financing our children's educations. Though it is unclear how much debt we will incur, we think our savings will be a good base and we will be able to manage our debt constructively. We have worked with financial advisors a little bit as we set up savings plans but have not relied on them for much college financial planning. As our children move into and through college, we will likely seek out financial plan-ners to help us understand how to effectively manage and efficiently pay off our debt.

With all this in mind, my advice to current and future parents is threefold. First, think about paying for college as an investment in your children's future, not as a bill you will eventually need to pay. Next, start planning for college as soon as you can, involving your children in conversations about financial planning over time. Finally, seek resources and counsel from folks knowledgeable about searching for colleges and financing a higher education, remembering that lots of good information is freely available.

The Sum of All Fears

"Can we afford college? How will we pay for it?" No two questions strike more terror in the hearts of parents and families than those. Most of the conversations I have about college with friends or families of prospective students do not begin with questions about academic majors or life on campus. They go straight to price. "Where can I find more information about scholarships? How much will we have to borrow to pay for college? Where can I get help with my financial aid application? We just aren't sure we can swing that price. If we choose this college for our daughter, we don't think we will have the resources to pay for our son's college later." And so on. Real questions, earnestly expressed, tinged with fear. The dream of sending children to the college of their choice, or even to college at all, often bumps uncomfortably against the reality of paying for it. This is true for families across the income spectrum. Worry spares no one.

Research bears out the anxiety. Poll data gathered by the Gallup organization indicate that affordability fears are widespread and pervasive. Nearly three-quarters of parents of school-age children today say they are worried about paying for college. They worry more about money for college than any other financial concern.[1] I see this at my own institutions. Six in ten parents of new entering students describe the financial aid their daughter or son received as the deciding factor in their enrollment decision. Another 30 percent say it is an important factor in their decision. Few say that financial aid did not matter. Different colleges would report different figures, but the bottom line is that most families feel, and have felt for some time, the squeeze of rising college prices.

The reasons driving the anxiety are not difficult to understand. Since 2007, the inflation-adjusted incomes of American families have declined for those with the lowest incomes, not grown at all for those in the middle, and risen by just 2 percent for families with above average, but not the highest, incomes. Only those with incomes in the highest 20 percent of all families have experienced significant income growth since 2007, and even there the growth is concentrated among the very highest-earning families.[2] While family incomes have declined or risen only slowly for most families, the price of college before financial aid has escalated mostly continuously at public and private colleges and universities across the country. Between 2007 and 2015, the inflation-adjusted average comprehensive price of attendance for all colleges in the United States (a figure that includes tuition, fees, room, and board) rose by nearly 23 percent.[3] Those figures are worthy of a stomach-churning gulp for most parents. In economic terms, it's eminently clear that the effort required to enroll in college has increased for families.

Concerns about price—*price sensitivity* in economic parlance—clearly influence the college choices students make today. Nearly 70 percent of families say that at some point in the admission process, they eliminated a college from consideration due to its cost. Fully half make that choice before applying, a frightening statistic for most colleges because they have no chance to put their best financial foot forward. Worse, but not surprising, the percentage of families who say they eliminate colleges from consideration based on price is rising.[4]

As a parent who will have children in college continuously from 2015 through 2028 (what were we thinking?), I'm acutely aware of the financial pressure associated with our kids' education. As a college professional, I also understand that the question has two edges: Who can afford to enroll at my institution and whom can my institution afford to enroll? All colleges understand that, which is why outlays for institutionally awarded scholarships and grants increased by 67 percent after adjusting for inflation between 2007 and 2016.[5] Financial aid is big business because affordability concerns are a big worry.

Educationomics 101

Fear and worry, however, do not constitute a plan. As you look ahead to your child's college education, take some time first to learn about price and cost, and then to develop a plan and parameters for making a college choice. Let's think about this as an imaginary interview.

Jon, we typically hear most about tuition, but what about other college costs? What kinds of total costs will my family really face?

Excellent question. Tuition and required fees represent only a portion of the costs your family will face when your child enrolls in college. You must also consider room and board (food) expenses—even if your child lives at home, they still have to eat—as well as textbooks and other miscellaneous day-to-day expenses. Though they typically receive far less attention than the price of tuition, nontuition expenses add up, representing nearly 30 percent of the average total price of attendance at private colleges and universities in 2016, approximately 55 percent of the price at public four-year colleges and universities, and 70 percent of the price at two-year colleges.[6] Most colleges award financial aid on the basis of the total cost of attendance, not just tuition. Textbook and other miscellaneous expenses typically are similar at different colleges. Not so for room and board. The geographic location of the college, as well as the style and quality of housing and food plans, drive significant variability in those costs from school to school. For purposes of planning, it's important that you pay close attention to both tuition and nontuition costs, which together make up the comprehensive price of attendance.

Why is college so expensive?

Nearly everyone asks this question, which is not surprising given the rate at which the price of college has increased over a long period of time. Though the terms *price* and *cost* are used interchangeably for convenience, their technical differences are important for both parents and colleges. The two terms are related, of course, but they aren't the same. One, price, reflects charges to students and families. Price represents what you will pay. The other, cost, represents the resources required by the college to deliver the experience. It's what appears in our budgets and on our financial balance sheets. We directly control some of our costs (like how much we choose to pay faculty and staff), while others are subject to external conditions (like utility costs).

Let's start with price. Colleges everywhere typically spend a lot of time each year reviewing their price. The decision to change price is never a casual one. Two factors exert strong influence on the price of attendance and the rate at which it changes from year to year:

- *The amount the college chooses to or needs to spend to provide its educational experience to the students it seeks to enroll.* No rocket science or deep math there. Like any business enterprise, colleges set their price at a level required to raise some portion of the total revenue necessary to deliver the experience they promise.

- *The level of subsidy the institution receives from nontuition sources.* Those subsidies come in various forms, but two are chiefly important. For public institutions, taxpayer appropriations often significantly reduce the price of attendance charged to students. In some cases, state legislators either set the price at public colleges or specify the rate at which it can change from year to year. Next, for public and private institutions alike, support from endowments (akin to a savings account) or the annual gifts of alumni help to underwrite the cost of the education and, as result, can influence the price charged—either directly in the form of a lower price or indirectly through increased financial aid.

A college's posted price of attendance is not the last word on pricing. All colleges award financial aid to their students, typically in the form of grants, scholarships, loans, and student employment, which can significantly reduce what families will actually pay. In the end, families confront the final price along two dimensions: objectively as an affordability question ("Do we actually have the resources required to pay for this experience for our son or daughter?") and subjectively as a value question ("Is this experience worth it at this price?"). Those questions are common to all consumer purchases; we make the same kind of judgments every time we buy something. What makes the college financial choice different from most other consumer choices is its size—for most families, only the purchase of a home carries a larger price tag than a college education for their children.

The highest-priced schools often receive a great deal of public attention, but keep in mind that college prices vary significantly. During the 2016–17 academic year, half of all students attending four-year colleges and universities in the United States were enrolled at schools with tuition under $12,000. Only one in eight students attended a school whose tuition exceeded $39,000 (though many of those institutions are among the most selective and well-known colleges in the world). In 2016–17, in-state tuition and fees at flagship public universities ranged from a low of $5,100 at West Virginia University to a high of $17,900 at Pennsylvania State University. Average tuition at community colleges was as low as $1,700 in New Mexico and as high as $7,700 in Vermont. And nearly half of all students attending private colleges are enrolled at schools with tuition below $33,000.[7] Financial aid awarded by all of those institutions, two-year and four-year, public and private, often reduces the price significantly for students. The point is, headlines notwithstanding, college costs cut across a wide range of price points, making it worth your time to explore your options.

So how are cost and price different?

At its simplest, price is what you pay for an experience, and cost is the value of the resources (human and physical) required to deliver it.[8] What you pay for college finances the costs required to produce the experience. That's pretty straightforward. However, the relationship of cost and price are different in higher education than they are for other products we buy. For example, when we buy a car, the basic financial equation sets cost equal to the price paid less the profit the auto manufacturer expects to claim. The price is explicitly higher than the cost. The same equation holds true for clothing, food, and nearly everything else we purchase. But in higher education, cost equals the price you pay plus a third-party subsidy (typically provided by taxpayers or donors). The price is less than the cost. Really. Price as a percentage of cost varies significantly among institutions, depending on the level of taxpayer support at public institutions and the level of wealth at private institutions. The more resources any college or university, public or private, can attract, the less dependent it will be on tuition to finance operational costs.

Fascinating as all that may be to those deeply interested in economics (and I count myself among that crowd), the explanation provides little practical insight into why costs at colleges are what they are. So I prefer to use imagery. Although it would be easy to compare cost structures at colleges to hospitals (they have many similarities in both cost structure and price) or, worse, to prisons (there actually are some similarities there, too), I think the most appropriate image is a small city. Colleges often enroll thousands of students, employ hundreds and sometimes thousands of faculty and staff, maintain hundreds of thousands of square feet of buildings and hundreds or thousands of acres of property, and provide an array of services that equal or exceed those available in small or even medium-sized cities.

Each of those pieces has a cost, often a significant cost. Expenditures at all colleges and universities in the United States totaled nearly $500 billion in 2014–15, or nearly 2.5 percent of the nation's gross domestic product.[9] The vast majority of those expenditures are for people. At my two institutions, both of them four-year liberal arts colleges, salaries and wages account for nearly 80 percent of our operating budget each year, a percentage that would be typical at many, and likely most, colleges and universities. People drive the enterprise: faculty, librarians, financial aid counselors, admissions representatives, information technology specialists, grounds and custodial crews, academic advisors, dining service staff, coaches, residence hall directors, fund-raising professionals, graduate assistants, and research fellows, among many others. American colleges and universities employ nearly four million people.[10] Each of these people has a part to play in delivering the college experience.

Individual colleges often have a hard time explaining their costs, partly because the language economists use to describe cost can be difficult to understand but more importantly because we too often retreat immediately to objects of expenditures (like the cost of technology or food or faculty salaries or fitness centers). In retreating to the details, we lose sight of the bigger—and more readily understandable—factors in play.

I think there's a simpler way for families to gain at least a basic understanding of college costs as they consider schools. The cost of education at any college or university is largely shaped by four factors:

- *Breadth.* How much does the college offer or provide? You can evaluate that by looking at the size of the curriculum (that is, how many courses, majors, and academic experiences the college supports), the variety of academic and student support services offered (like academic advising, counseling and health services, information technology resources, and career advising), and the range of residential and student life programming it provides (including athletics). At many institutions, the menu of curricular and cocurricular options, as well as the services that support student success, are extensive. Each must be staffed and funded.

- *Depth.* Within that broad array of offerings, how many choices or options does the college provide? All colleges offer academic majors, for example, but within a major, how many tracks or course options does the school provide? How many study abroad experiences does it support? How deeply does the institution support academic advising, personal health counseling, or athletics?

The breadth and depth of the programs and services a college provides define its experience and shape its cost structure.

- *Scale.* Most simply, scale reflects bigness or smallness. How are the costs associated with the breadth and depth of the experience the college provides spread across its students? Costs allocated across many students often result in a lower cost per student (more common at large institutions), while costs spread across fewer students typically indicate a higher cost per student (characteristic at small institutions). The student-to-faculty ratio provides a common way of evaluating scale. Smaller ratios of students to faculty (say, ten to one) typically indicate higher costs than higher ratios (like fifteen to one). But scale is more than a mathematical reflection of large and small. It also reflects the choices and values of the school. All colleges and universities, regardless of their size, make judgments about the scale at which they want to offer their experience. Some choose an explicitly "small and deep is beautiful" approach—in economic terms providing a high level of inputs per student, which almost always results in higher costs per student. Others choose an approach defined by a kind of mass production, fewer units of input per student, the classic definition of efficiency and one that often yields lower costs per student.

- *Level of investment.* How much does the school invest in its people, experiences, and operations? Level of investment is an anchor, framing how a college or university manages and delivers the breadth, depth, and scale of the experiences it provides. Some investments are easier to spot than others. A well-maintained campus, for example, often reflects significant capital investment in facilities. Similarly, higher-paid faculty or wide and deep program offerings signal high levels of operational investment in the collegiate experience. Revenue is the prime mover shaping cost and level of investment. In higher education, cost often is shaped less by technology, wages, or an objective assessment of need than by the amount of revenue available to spend.[11] More revenue provides more opportunity for spending. Even though high levels of investment do not uniformly indicate a quality experience, or even the right experience for every student, it's no accident that most college rankings sort schools based on resource wealth. The most highly rated schools nearly always also have the largest resource base and the deepest level of investment.

These factors are important. Together they define the experience the college provides, and they shape its value. They clearly are interdependent and reflect a vast array of choices at institutions large and small. You needn't be an economist or a financial analyst to gather enough information by observation or a few well-placed questions to understand enough about any of them to gain at least a working knowledge of the cost structure (and its supporting price) at any particular school. Having gathered that information, you will need to make a judgment about what you value most.

Will college prices likely continue to rise?

The short answer is yes, at most institutions, though likely much more slowly than they did a decade ago. Price-setting typically is a time-consuming exercise at colleges and universities. Yet in spite of the lengthy conversations and mathematical modeling that drive and define the price-setting process, it often yields a consistent and similar outcome across the marketplace. Simply put, similar types of institutions, particularly those competing in the same geographic regions for the same students, typically raise their prices at similar rates and land on similar comprehensive prices. The prices and price changes do not reflect shared planning or, worse, collusion, but instead result from common cost structures and pressures and a common understanding of the students they seek to enroll. Over a long period of time, most colleges and universities have learned what types of students and families have been able and willing to consider their educational experience. In other words, price setting often reflects a behavior born of understanding and familiarity: particular kinds of students and families will seek particular kinds of colleges and universities within a particular range of prices. That market experience often is shared among many institutions.

Public and private institutions set price differently, though the purpose of price-setting is similar at both. In addition to considerations of markets and cost structures, price at public colleges and universities also is shaped by levels of taxpayer support and the level of price control exercised by public policy makers, both of which vary considerably by state and even by institutional systems within states. Sharp declines in state appropriations for higher education in recent years often resulted in steep tuition rate increases at public colleges and universities as those institutions sought to recoup at least a portion of their lost revenue. However, few public institutions have the autonomous flexibility to raise their price as they see fit in response to changes in state appropriations without legislative approval or input. Legislative pressures often act as a constraint on the ability of leaders at public colleges and universities to raise their price of attendance (at least for in-state students). Private colleges and universities, on the other hand, generally do not receive direct operating subsidies from taxpayers and are not subject to legislative oversight on price. They must engage the marketplace directly when they set price—also a risky proposition given that their starting price position most often is higher than it is at public institutions. In either case, though, both public and private colleges work to set a price designed to successfully enroll the students they seek and to generate the resources they need to effectively serve those students.

As pressure mounts both externally and internally to control college costs and reimagine the college experience, I'm convinced we will see more price experimentation in the coming years, particularly among schools that find themselves most at economic risk. "Are we priced appropriately to the students we seek to enroll? Can we continue to raise our price at this rate? Does our price point provide us with an opportunity to generate the resources we need to operate as we expect? Can we afford to behave like everybody else in the marketplace? How are we positioned for the future?" These are questions college and university leaders commonly ask. They surely will be posed with increasing frequency and urgency over the next decade. What might the answers look like? That's not yet clear, though strategies like tuition reductions, tuition freezes, more highly differentiated pricing by program or activity (including things like housing and amenities), and even greater increases in student financial aid all will receive more attention.

You've mentioned financial aid several times. Explain how that works. It seems complex and even scary.

Families pay for college using two types of their own current resources: income and savings. You should expect to use some combination of those two to pay for your son or daughter's college experience.

But income and savings often are not enough to finance a college education, and that's where financial aid comes into play.

At its simplest, financial aid is intended to fill the gap between what families can afford to pay (as determined by their financial aid application) and the price of the college. It comes in three basic forms: grants and scholarships, loans, and student employment (or work-study). Though not typically understood or presented as financial aid, federal tax benefits for education also help families offset their college costs.

For all its importance, the process of applying for financial aid can appear labyrinthine and daunting. The terms that define it often make it difficult to understand. For example, grants and scholarships directly reduce the price of attendance at a college, but they are awarded differently. Grants typically are awarded on the basis of ability to pay, derived from the financial aid application. Scholarships, on the other hand, are awarded independently of a family's ability to pay and most often are based on academic, artistic, or athletic achievement. Similarly, some loans are based on a family's ability to pay, others not. Some can be taken out by the student himself or herself, while others require a credit-worthy cosigner. Many websites dedicate themselves to explaining financial aid, among them National Association of Student Financial Aid Administrators (nasfaa.org), BigFuture (bigfuture.collegeboard.org), and FinAid (finaid.org). They can provide helpful information as you begin your planning process.

The financial aid process itself begins with an application for aid. The financial aid application will determine your family's ability to pay, and thus your eligibility for need-based grants, loans, and work-study funding. Nearly all colleges use the FAFSA as their primary financial aid application form, though many of those same institutions either request additional financial information not collected on the FAFSA or require completion of an additional financial aid form.

Aid application forms are complex and foreign to many families, and the formulas used to determine ability to pay seem, and in many ways are, both mysterious and arcane. My conversations with families suggest that most fill out their college financial aid applications with equal measures of fear and faith and little sense of understanding about what the completed process might actually yield. They cross their fingers and hope for the best.

At its simplest, financial need reflects the difference between a family's ability to pay (which is derived from information about family income, family assets, family size, and the number of children in college) and the total price of attendance at a school, including tuition, fees, room, board, and other college-going costs. In theory, though not always in practice, ability to pay remains the same irrespective of the college your student chooses to attend. If I have an ability to pay of $10,000 at the University of X, then I should have the same or similar ability to pay at the College of Y, independent of the price of either. My financial need varies among the various institutions to which I apply for admission only because the price of attendance varies.

On paper these practices seem neat and straightforward. In reality they more often are sources of extraordinary anxiety, especially as the price of college rises. Financial aid professionals at all types of institutions can tell tales of families who believe they need at least some assistance to pay for college, in spite of the ability-to-pay numbers that tumble out of the financial aid application process. Those stories are easy to understand when the price of sending even one child to college represents an enormous share of family income.

Like federal and state income tax rates, expected ability to pay for college goes up as family income and wealth increase. No magic there. The formulas are progressive; the more resources you have, the more you will be expected to pay for college (all other things remaining equal, of course). Financial aid formulas effectively identify families with little ability to pay for college, the families who should and most often do receive the greatest assistance. However, because the expectations built into the formulas become more steeply progressive for families with incomes over about $75,000, they create fear among families who would otherwise describe themselves as middle-class or even upper middle-class.

As you approach the college admission process, you should never hesitate to ask questions of the financial aid office. They not only will explain terms and timelines; they also can guide you through the application process step-by-step. You will be asked to share detailed information about your family income and assets. Those conversations are deeply personal and maybe even uncomfortable. But in the case of paying for college, they are especially important. The information you provide can mean the difference of thousands of dollars annually and can influence the types of college options your daughter or son may have.

Who gets financial aid? What are our chances of getting aid?

The vast majority of college students in the United States today receive some form of financial aid to help them pay for school. According to US Department of Education data, 83 percent of all first-time, full-time new students in 2014–15 received financial aid assistance in the form of grants, scholarships, loans, or work-study (sometimes all of them). The number and percentage of students receiving financial aid has risen steadily and significantly since 2000.[12] The amount of financial aid awarded to undergraduate students across the country is staggering, totaling nearly $200 billion in 2015–16—a sum that reflects grants, scholarships, loans, work-study, and tax credits. Two-thirds of all financial aid comes from three sources: federal Pell Grants (exclusively awarded based on ability to pay), federal loans, and institutional grants and scholarships.[13] For many students and families, financial aid is what makes college attendance possible.

Across all new entering students at all colleges and universities in the United States in 2014–15, 45 percent received a federal grant, 33 percent a state or local grant, 43 percent a grant or scholarship awarded by their school, and 47 percent borrowed. The likelihood of assistance varies considerably by type of institution. Among new students who enrolled at private four-year colleges and universities, 82 percent received an institutionally awarded grant or scholarship, compared to 47 percent at public four-year colleges and universities. On the other hand, 61 percent of new private college students took out a federal student loan, compared to 50 percent of new public college students. You should examine both the availability of financial aid and the distribution of financial aid at the colleges to which your daughter or son applies. Schools routinely post that kind of information on their websites. It will help you understand more about the types and amounts of aid you may be eligible to receive.

Grants and scholarships do not need to be repaid. Nor, unlike student employment, do they need to be earned throughout the year. They typically are awarded at the beginning of an academic year, often for multi-year periods. Not surprisingly, they are the most sought-after form of financial aid. Keep in mind that some colleges award only need-based grants—based on information about ability to pay collected on the FAFSA. Those schools do not award scholarships based on academic achievement or other nonfinancial criteria. They target their aid exclusively to students with the least ability to pay.

But many schools, public and private, offer both need-based grants and scholarships based on academic or creative achievement. Scholarship awards often are granted categorically, meaning that everyone who meets the criteria for the award receives it. They are offered independent of a family's ability to pay and may or may not require completion of a financial aid application. Grant and scholarship awarding practices vary significantly from college to college. What earns you a grant or scholarship at one school may not at another. To learn more about grants and scholarships awarded at a specific college, consult the school's website or call its financial aid office. Never assume that an award you receive at one institution will be similarly awarded at another.

Finally, know that financial aid is a scarce resource at all colleges and universities. Schools use a variety of formulas to award need-based and achievement-based aid in order to manage how much money they spend, often finely targeting who receives the aid. They do that to simultaneously achieve both enrollment and budget goals, a complex proposition as demands to improve affordability (meaning more financial aid) often clash with demands for improvement in the collegiate experience (meaning more spending). That battle requires trade-offs, and all colleges make them.

I always advise students and families to call the financial aid office with questions they have about their eligibility for financial aid, as well as questions about the types of aid for which they may be eligible. Financial aid offices everywhere are set up to answer those kinds of questions.

How should we think about student loans and borrowing? Stories about student debt levels are frightening.

In 2013, the Federal Reserve Bank of New York released a report indicating that for the first time, total outstanding student loan balances for all borrowers approached $1 trillion[14]—a figure since surpassed. The data reflected loan balances for those currently enrolled in school as undergraduate or graduate students, as well as those no longer enrolled, representing millions of borrowers of all ages. The finer details of the calculation notwithstanding, by any reckoning, $1 trillion is a staggering figure. It's no surprise that stories of ruinous student indebtedness have become a staple of news journalism. After the price of college, no other higher education statistic draws as much public attention or creates as much anguish as rising student debt.

But not everyone borrows. In 2014–15, nearly four in ten bachelor's degree recipients from public and private not-for-profit colleges and universities completed college without having taken out a student loan. Among those who did borrow, the average cumulative amount borrowed totaled just over $28,000. Although large debt burdens receive a great deal of attention, most students who take out student loans borrow less than $20,000, and 40 percent borrow less than $10,000 to pay for college.[15] Amounts borrowed vary considerably by type of college attended and, to be sure, some students and families borrow extraordinary amounts to finance their undergraduate education. But the bleak picture painted in popular stories does not accurately represent reality for most student borrowers.

Many people ask, "Should my daughter or son take out a student loan? Should we borrow to help pay for their college? How much should we borrow?" Unfortunately, there is no one-size-fits-all answer to those important questions. But there are a number of important considerations to keep in mind as you wrestle with them:

- Borrowing can greatly expand your college options, allowing your son or daughter to consider a wider range of colleges. Student loans provide access to resources beyond what you may have available with current income or savings and fill gaps after scholarships and grants. That said, like any other form of capital borrowing, student or parent loans should be considered in the context of what you expect in return. Do you value the collegiate experience enough to borrow up to a certain level? Only you can answer that question, but you do need to ask it.

- The type of loan matters. Different loans carry different interest rates and different repayment terms. Without doubt, federal student loans offer the lowest rates and the most flexible repayment options. Private loans typically are less flexible than federal loans and nearly always require a creditworthy cosigner, meaning that you or someone close to your family will agree to take on the obligation of repayment in the event your daughter or son cannot meet their repayment obligations. They also typically come with a high interest rate.

- Monthly payments on student loans typically total approximately 1 percent of the principal amount borrowed, meaning that a student who borrowed $20,000 could expect to pay about $200 per month during repayment. You should think about that in the context of anticipated postcollege earnings.

- Though almost never framed this way, borrowing is an entitlement—which makes it both an attractive and a dangerous financing option. If you are eligible for a loan (or a loan of a particular size), you can access it. The choice is wholly yours. Colleges do not force students to borrow nor do they have the power to tell students and families that they cannot borrow. With that in mind, as a rule of thumb, borrow only what you need. We college professionals see too many families in our financial aid offices who borrow too much simply because they can, not because they have to or they should. If what you need to borrow to finance your daughter or son's education goes beyond either your comfort or your financial limits, then it is best to consider a different college option.

Student loans are a key piece of the college financing puzzle for many families, representing nearly one-third of the total financial aid received by undergraduate students nationally. Popular news stories that demonize borrowing notwithstanding, answers to questions about how much students should borrow for college or whether all students should be subject to the same borrowing limits are not at all clear. Unlike most other forms of borrowing, which typically require a physical form of collateral, the only collateral required for most student loans (those not cosigned by parents or someone else) is the student's future prospects. They represent an investment in the future. Like any other investment, the decision to borrow should be considered carefully and wisely.

From Hope to Action

In early 2007, my brother called to tell me that he and his family would be featured in a lead story on the *CBS Evening News*. That sounded ominous. Lead stories usually feature conflict, disaster, and mayhem of all kinds. Thankfully, we didn't have to worry about any of those ugly topics. The subject of the story was, however, both uncomfortable and important. My brother's family was part of a feature piece headlined, "Savings at Lowest Rate Since Depression,"[16] which highlighted a government report indicating that the US savings rate for the prior year was negative—that is, people had tapped into their savings to support or meet their expenses. Robert Samuelson, economics correspondent for the *Washington Post* and *Newsweek*, noted in the story that people were spending and not saving because the economy was so good. Though his comment was not offered as a prognostication, in less than a year the economy would be in the deepest slump since the Great Depression.

My brother's family was selected by the program's producers to broadly represent American families everywhere. I had to think carefully then about whether it was a good thing or a bad thing that members of my family were chosen to represent Americans' struggle to save. In the end, though, my sister-in-law surely captured the sentiments and experiences of many then and now: "We're not the Rockefellers, but we're doing just fine. [But] I'm constantly asking myself, 'Hey wait a minute, how come we're running out of money at the end of the month?'"

In an ideal world, like the ant in Aesop's fable *The Grasshopper and the Ant*, families everywhere would take the opportunity to look beyond the pressures and pleasures of today to prepare for the necessities and opportunities of tomorrow. Although the work of Aesop's ant was grueling, the basic message is down-home and straightforward: preparing for tomorrow is a good and wise thing to do. Unfortunately, the reality of the present often intervenes, undermining the best intentions to plan. Too often we are a nation of "hopers," not planners. Unfortunately, hope is not a strategy.

Most people understand the value of financial planning for college. That's an important first step. Nearly nine in ten parents with children under age 18 agree that having a plan to pay for college is important, though most also agree that it is challenging to create a plan and believe that it is more difficult to save and pay for college today than it used to be.[17] Financing fears aside, families are committed to providing their children with a high-quality college experience (however they choose to define "high quality"). Two-thirds of all parents agree that "giving my child the ideal college experience, regardless of cost, is important to me." That commitment was not limited to families of the highest means; it reached across all incomes.

Understanding the value of financial planning is one thing. Acting on it is another. Only half of parents with school-age children indicate they actually have a plan to pay for college. The reasons many cite for not planning are straightforward: "We can't afford to save, our children are too young" (a variation of "We don't need to worry about it yet"), "We need help creating a plan, or we don't know how to save."[18] My experience has been that many families approach paying for college as a current expense—mostly by expecting to rely on their income—rather than as something to be planned and financed over a much longer period of time. Unfortunately, the reality is that college often is a large expense for families. If you have more than one child, it absolutely is a large expense.

Creating a financial plan can be a daunting experience, and not everyone has the resources to seek professional help to prepare one. Still, hewing to a few simple considerations can take you a long way.

Save. It's timeless advice. A penny saved is a penny earned. It's not about how much money you make, it's how you save it. Spending is what's left after saving. Save money, and money will save you. And so on. Aphorisms are easy to come by. The practice of saving is considerably more difficult for most people. Our culture values immediate wants over longer-term needs—a fact made clear by the torrent of retail advertising that pervades every form of media. Saving requires habit, demanding forethought over impulse. It's easy to put off. More importantly, life has a way of intervening that threatens or derails even the best-laid plans. A lost job or reduction in pay, unexpected medical expenses, or just the cost of everyday life—food, housing, transportation—often conspire to limit our ability to save or our interest in saving.

The news about savings in America isn't great. Research by the Federal Reserve Board on the well-being of households in 2015 found that two-thirds of all people who are not retired say that they save something—good news. However, among those who do save, four in ten reported saving an amount equal to less than 5 percent of their income, and two-thirds said they saved the equivalent of less than 10 percent of their income.[19] A CNBC news report in 2017 laid it out in stark terms: the vast majority of Americans have under $1,000 saved and half of all Americans have nothing at all put away for retirement. Only 15 percent of all Americans surveyed reported that they had more than $10,000 in their savings accounts.[20] The bottom line: most families are prepared neither for retirement nor for college expenses. Crushing debt is not a forgone conclusion with college-going.

My friend Chris Farrell (who wrote this book's foreword) is Senior Economics Contributor for American Public Media's Marketplace Radio. He not only offers savvy financial advice; he does it in a way that is easy to understand. I asked him about how families should prepare financially for college, and this is what he said:

> A college degree is a passport to better employment opportunities over a lifetime. The cost of paying for that college degree can also be mind boggling. But don't buy into the fear. For one thing, many families don't pay the full price of college. For another, you don't need to have saved the total tab. Setting aside a quarter to a third of the college bill is enough to ease the strain on household finances. The goal is for your student to graduate from college with as little debt as possible, and savings will limit how much your child will borrow.

The ability to save is hardly a constant, though. It varies with the stages of our life, personal and professional. In theory, it is simplest when our lives are simplest, like before we have children or own homes or need to purchase automobiles. But those times generally occur just as we begin our adult years and working careers and thus have the fewest resources available to save. As we get older, perhaps earning more, the expenses associated with our lives get more complicated, also making it difficult to put resources aside. The problem from the vantage point of paying for college is that savings represent an important leg of the three-legged family financial stool (the other two being current income and debt). Saving for college can reduce financial anxiety and expand school options. With that in mind, Chris Farrell offered this practical advice: "It pays to keep it simple and start small. The most effective way to boost savings over time is to make it automatic. Have your financial institution automatically shift a few dollars from your checking account into college savings every month. You can always increase the amount you save as your pay increases."

The ability to save will influence the college opportunities your children will have. In 2016, nearly six in ten parents with school-age children reported that they were saving for college, up sharply from the prior three years and a welcome reversal of trend.[21] Those who said they were saving for college were three times more confident in their ability to meet the costs of their children's higher education than those who did not save. Edna Mode, the delightfully eccentric superhero costume designer in the Disney/Pixar movie *The Incredibles*, said simply as she was preparing the hero protagonists for action, "Luck favors the prepared." Though luck may not be the right sentiment in this case, her admonition is spot on: college opportunity favors those who have saved.

One persistent myth often influences the choices people make about whether to save for their child's college education—that saving for college damages the ability to receive financial aid. The presumption is that savings will make a family look wealthier, thereby limiting the ability to receive need-based grants. That logic is simply wrong. Financial aid formulas protect a significant amount of family savings from assessment of ability to pay for college—appropriately recognizing that families need to save for more than education. The maximum assessment rate on savings built into federal financial aid needs analysis is less than six cents on the dollar. In other words, for most families, saving for college has relatively little impact on the ability-to-pay calculation. The most common reward for choosing not to save is the opportunity to borrow more, a choice that simply substitutes one form of payment (saving) for another (future income).

My advice for saving, the blueprint my wife and I followed for our four children, is simple, but it does require a discipline spread out over many years:

- Use the advantages of time and compound interest as your friend. If you start with an initial investment of $100 at a child's birth, and then save just $25 per month, earning interest compounded monthly at even 4 percent, you will have nearly $8,000 in hand at the point your child enrolls in college, enough to finance books and expenses for four years (at least in present-day dollars). Double the monthly amount to $50, and you will have more than $15,000 when your child begins college. The point is to get into the habit of saving as early as possible. Putting money away always involves trade-offs, a consideration of the known present against an unknown future. But it is remarkable how fast eighteen years go by—just ask a parent who has been there, wondering how their small child suddenly became a young adult. Even small investments made early can yield significant sums later on.

- Make a plan based on a realistic assessment of what you can afford, hold yourself to it, and periodically review your plan. You do not need to save in relation to the total cost of college, a sum that mostly frightens people and serves as a disincentive to save. Smaller, realistic goals often work best. When we began to have children, my wife and I set a goal to try to save a percentage of current college prices (we assumed about 30 percent of the price), hoping that the rate of interest on those savings would grow at a rate at least similar to the growth in college prices—a gamble that actually paid off. You could also set a numeric goal or target. In either case, setting a goal is helpful and allows you to see progress. Saving something, anything, is better than saving nothing at all.

- Take the time to explore the federal tax-advantaged savings vehicles available to you and your family, like 529 plans and Coverdell Education Savings Accounts (more commonly known as Education IRAs). Each offers the opportunity to earn interest tax-free for qualified college expenses. The requirements of the plans differ (and you should read the fine print), but both can be opened with little money (less than $100) and provide opportunities for significant contributions over many years. Offered by every state, as well as independently, 529 plans are contributory—meaning other family members or friends can deposit funds into them, a useful substitute for toys quickly forgotten at holidays and birthdays. This gift keeps on giving. You can learn more about college savings plan options at websites like FinAid (finaid.org) or Saving for College (savingforcollege.com). I always encourage young families to explore and consider tax-advantaged college savings accounts.

Define Value

No matter your family's ability to pay for college, think carefully about what you are willing to pay for it. What kind of experience do you value enough to pay for? For what kind of college or college experience would you be willing to stretch your resources? Planning and saving for college improves your ability to pay for it. A sense of value seals the deal. We make judgments about value all the time, from the most mundane of purchases (like chocolates) to the most complex (like cars or houses). In his insightful book, *The Paradox of Choice*, Swarthmore College psychology professor Barry Schwartz takes on the vast array of choices we face in a modern consumer economy. He offers advice that is as applicable to a decision about which college to attend as it is to the purchase of a car: sort out your goals, evaluate the importance of each goal, and evaluate how your options help you to meet your goals.[22] Of course, assessing value also requires assessing risk—and that's important when making a college choice because the result cannot be known in advance of the experience and in any case plays out over the decades that follow. Even in the absence of knowing the future, it remains important to ask whether the risk of stretching your family resources for a particular college or college experience is worth the reward or value your children see in that school or experience.

For nearly all families, resources are finite. It's fun to dream, but reality typically intervenes at the point of purchase. Defining value and considering risk helps us to understand not only what we are buying but why we are buying it. Are you willing to pay more for something (within the limits of your resources) if you think it's worth it—that is, if it delivers clear value or an advantage in relation to the price of some other similar product or service? It's Beats vs. Bose. Talk with your college-bound children about value—asking them what they value most and why, and asking yourself what you are willing to pay to support it. All colleges come with lots of bells, whistles, and pledges of excellence. You should take the time to sort out which matter most to you and to your son or daughter.

Know Your Limits

How much is too much, if you have to stretch financially? That's a key question and one families should not ignore as their children engage the college admission process. Nationally, nearly one-quarter of families say that the price of attendance (after the receipt of financial aid) is the deciding factor in their final choice.[23] At my own institutions, both private colleges, 70 percent of parents said that the cost to their family after financial aid was a "very important" factor in their daughter or son's final choice. More than four in ten described their financial aid award as the deciding factor at the point of selection. Net price after financial aid was cited as a concern by families of all incomes.

Despite your perceptions of the quality or value of a college, you do need to understand your financial limits—the amount that forms the outer boundary of your ability to pay. This is true for all families, but particularly those with more than one child. As parents of four children, my wife and I have had to consider the price of attendance not one at a time, but rather across all four simultaneously. It's a delicate financial balancing act, ensuring that each will have the opportunity to access the collegiate experience best for them. The amount we choose to spend in support of one of our children has implications for what we will have available for those who follow.

I never advise students or families to reject a college out of hand, before application, simply because of its posted price of attendance. Until you complete the financial aid process, you won't know how much you will pay, and in many cases financial aid makes the net price of more expensive institutions less than the price at schools with lower posted costs of attendance. Still, begin the process with the end in mind and have at least a general idea of a net price point that works for your family. We see too many families in our financial aid offices who did not make that calculation. They often struggle financially throughout their son or daughter's college years—stretched beyond their limits (which often results in extraordinary pressure to borrow) but fearful of disrupting their child's college experience. Those tales are often heart-wrenching for schools, students, and families alike.

Talk with Your Kids about Money

Let them know how much you can and will provide to support their college education and what you expect they will provide on their own.

Conversations about money and family resources rival talks about sex in terms of parental discomfort. "We just can't pay that" often comes out (unnecessarily) as a confession of guilt. For most families today, the college admission process involves providing minutely detailed family financial information to a financial aid office. My experience has been that though students may have an idea about their family's financial wherewithal, most have little more than a shadowy understanding. Regardless of their socioeconomic status, teenagers typically judge their family's income in relation to the way they live their lives on a daily basis—often through their food, housing, clothing, and access to life experiences, none of which may paint a complete picture. Each fall, my office surveys our new entering students, asking them to broadly estimate their parents' income. We then analyze what they said in relation to the actual income data provided by their parents on the financial aid application. Year in and year out, our students are as likely to overestimate their parents' income as they are to underestimate it. Most simply don't know.

Given the cost of college today, "the money talk" is more important than ever. Talk with your children about how you will define and assess value. Let them know in advance about the limits of your ability to pay. Be clear about your expectations of them, how much you expect they will contribute each year from their own earnings and savings. Perhaps most of all, talk in advance about the role of debt in paying for their college, including debt both they and you will incur. These conversations may not yield a magically happy result—they mostly serve to define limits. But both for your own financial security and theirs, defining those limits before they get to college is a key step in managing the choice.

FIVE
Choose

Congratulations!
Today is your day.
You're off to Great Places!
You're off and away! . . .
You'll look up and down streets. Look 'em over with care.
About some you will say, "I don't choose to go there."
With your head full of brains and your shoes full of feet,
you're too smart to go down any not-so-good street. . . .
Oh! The places you'll go!
—Dr. Seuss, *Oh, the Places You'll Go!*

 From Rodney Morrison, Associate Provost for Enrollment and Retention Management, Stony Brook University, New York

Dear Parents,

Because I have spent most of my professional career in college admissions, my three children have virtually grown up on college campuses. I recently asked my middle- and high school–aged children for their opinions on college and the college admission process. Rather than telling me what they thought, they instead described what their friends thought—a true teen response. They reported that their friends, and especially the parents of their friends, assumed that my kids already knew everything about the college search process and would not need to worry because their father has "connections." Their friends also assumed our family would plan better for college and that we would experience no anxiety or frustration. Deep breath. I said that I did not know everything about college admission, that my "connections" would not drive their school search, and that our emotional ups and downs would be the same as those of any other family.

We keep a pile of college mail on the dinner table in our home, and my children often review and rank the brochures they like best and least. One winner provided a vibrant picture of a school against its urban background. It was an evening shot with lots of colors. Another mailer received mixed reviews: four students surrounded by grass and trees—"Beautiful, even though it was staged." My children have different personalities, and I've learned to expect that what appeals to them varies with their personalities. That's an important parental takeaway.

What has proven most important in our family is that my younger middle school daughters have felt a part of their high school big brother's college search process. All three of my children have already been to college fairs and visited a number of campuses—not to choose a particular school but to learn what college is like. Those visits have generated terrific conversations about different types of schools and the value of college. My advice: it's never too early to talk and dream.

 From Kaya Henderson, Chancellor (Retired), Washington, DC, Public Schools

Dear Parents,

Don't freak out, like I did, when in the midst of the application process during senior year, your child tells you, "I think I don't want to go to college." As the chancellor (superintendent) of Washington, DC, public schools, that was the absolute last thing I ever expected to hear from my oldest. Immediately, I thought I had failed as both a parent and an educator. I imagined my friends and colleagues shaking their heads about me working so hard to get other people's children to college but not tending my own garden. I was devastated.

My oldest was a kid who grew up in a college-oriented household. He began hearing about and visiting colleges and universities in elementary school. His middle school class was called the class of 2018—the projected year of their college graduation. We have basketball season tickets to the Georgetown University Hoyas. We did homework together as he was completing his sophomore year in high school and I was completing a master's degree. During his junior year, he participated in the Upward Bound program at Howard University in Washington, where he took classes each Saturday on Howard's campus and spent the summers living in the dorms, coming home only on weekends. Every time we took a family trip, we visited local college campuses. He had taken various AP classes and SAT prep courses. This was a young man who had been exposed early to college and for whom college expectations were high and clear. So I did not understand the words coming out of his mouth when he shared this incredible news.

He went on to explain that the cost-benefit analysis just didn't add up to him. First, he shared that the amount he would have to borrow to finance college at his top choices would be economically crippling in the long term. I explained that that was "the American way," and that he would get a job and pay off his student loans (eventually). He countered that many of his friends who were recent college grads were unemployed. He didn't want to end up on anyone's couch. He asked if we would consider a different proposal that would still lead to college. "Of course," replied my mouth, while my mind was thinking, "Hell, no!"

His proposal: join the military. During his sophomore year in high school, he had taken an Army ROTC class as the only elective that would fit his schedule. He enjoyed the structure, discipline, and leadership opportunities in ROTC so much that when the subsequent ROTC courses didn't fit into his class schedule, he went to school ninety minutes early each day to participate in a before-school ROTC class. He rose through the ranks, participated in citywide and regional competitions, and was transformed from a shy, quiet, and insecure boy into a confident young leader charting his own path in the world. He admitted that he wasn't exactly ready for college and that military service could help prepare him. He would be able to explore different careers and disciplines in the military to help determine exactly what he wanted to study. He'd be gaining skills and knowledge that would help him in college. Most importantly, military service would help pay for college and guarantee him a job when he finished. I had to admit that it wasn't a bad proposal—thorough, thoughtful, and still focused on college, just not right away.

We supported his ambitions, and months later we watched him begin his journey as an airman in the US Air Force. I was proud to see him serve our country, but even prouder of his educational journey. The kid who "wasn't exactly ready for college" attacked the learning opportunities offered to him in the Air Force. During his training, I watched him develop study habits that had eluded him in high school. After exploring his first interest, cybersecurity, he was offered the chance to try his hand at a medical career, given his high school experience in biotechnology. He decided to pursue a job in radiology and prepared for it by taking multiple anatomy, physiology, biology, and other courses. He pushed himself each time to score higher on his exams, so he could attain higher ranks and better pay. He had found the learning environment where he could excel. I realized that each of us has our own pathway.

My amazing son just completed his second year in the US Air Force, where he works in the radiology laboratory at Joint Base Andrews, southeast of Washington. He lives on base, has traveled extensively, earned his associate's degree, bought his first car, and saved quite a bit of money. He recently decided to begin applying to colleges to finish his bachelor's degree and is considering master's degree programs. He plans to return to the Air Force to take advantage of new career and leadership opportunities after completing his degrees. He's even talking about pursuing a PhD. I could not be more proud.

Our jobs, as parents and educators, is to raise well-adjusted, confident people who can make their way successfully in the world. It took mine rejecting our plan for his postsecondary experience to realize that we'd accomplished exactly what we'd set out to do.

✉ **From Scott Friedhoff, Vice President for Enrollment and College Relations, The College of Wooster, Ohio**

Dear Parents,

My wife and I have two sons. We knew from years of personal and professional experience that teenagers often lack the background knowledge to create their initial list of colleges. They simply aren't aware of the tremendous variety of colleges around the country and typically have not thought much about their own learning styles or needs. As our boys began their college search, my wife and I agreed that we would help guide its initial stages.

We focused initially on helping them to think about their abilities and interests. Our sons are utterly different from each other, although both were involved in a number of high school activities. Each liked challenging classes that were interactive and engaging. Those factors led us to help them create an initial list of colleges where they could continue to pursue their activities and interests (and discover new ones) and take full advantage of discussion-based classes. Their lists included traditional, residential liberal arts colleges. The boys looked to web tools that helped them evaluate their chances of both getting in and fitting in. Each wanted to find a school where he would be neither the best- nor the worst-prepared student. As they used those criteria to construct their initial lists, I knew that any place they selected would be fine.

We visited many schools. We tried to keep the visits to just one day, but that was not always easy. Convenience played a role in the colleges we visited. Given all the activities our boys were involved in, our visits often were planned at the last minute and required that we drive. That resulted in a set of visits that typically were within an eight-hour drive of our home. Through the course of our travels, we discovered what people frequently say about college visits: everything begins to blur when seeing too many too quickly. It becomes difficult to tell one institution from another or to remember what happened at one or another. Still, the visits were important and helped our sons winnow and refine their lists.

I watched both boys keep schools on their list or take them off for a mixture of sound reasons ("It was just too urban"), frustrating reasons

("I didn't like the tour guide"), and even curious reasons ("I liked how the dorms were lined up the hill and how you lived in a higher one as you progressed from first year to senior year"). Regardless of my own impressions of their reasoning, they each were drawing their own judgments and coming to their own conclusions—a win for any parent. In the end, both selected terrific schools that fit well for each—each seven hours away, in opposite directions!

Focus

I had a conversation with some friends whose daughter, a high school senior, was busily preparing her college applications. A top student at her school, she had approached her college search with a military-style discipline and focus, defining her interests and identifying and visiting schools across the country every chance she got. She's the kind of student that colleges dream about: smart, an accomplished musician, president of the student council, and active in myriad activities in and out of school. She planned to apply to more than a dozen schools. But after more than a year of planning to get to the point of college application, when I asked them about the schools she most preferred and why, they said she loved them all and had not yet figured out how she would make her choice. Where students will go to college—the aspirational and interesting part of the admission process—too often overwhelms the harder part: How they will sort the choices they have created for themselves, particularly if many of those choices are similar?

The tactics guiding the work of admissions offices by necessity are shaped by the needs and interests of the college. How many students do they seek to enroll or need to enroll? What kinds of students do they seek to enroll? What are their financial needs and limits? At most colleges, recruitment is built around a cycle, typically described as a funnel, of prospect-to-applicant-to-admitted-to-enrolled student. That cycle plays out over two and sometimes even three years. It's a highly goal-oriented, deadline-driven process. The results are measured by numbers. As it unfolds, the colleges where we professionals work don't generally have time to reflect on the information or values or feelings that matter most at each stage of the selection process, or how students and families understand and experience us, or why students ultimately select us. The traditional admission funnel defines recruitment workflow and structure. It provides a useful method for organizing a complex and lengthy process. Admissions offices need that structure to manage their time, resources, and energy. But it doesn't describe how students and families make their final choice.

A simple way to imagine the admission process is to think of it as a series of steps that consider your daughter or son's changing information needs and expectations at each point along the way. Regardless of the college experience they seek, students and families typically make their college choice in three stages, each building on the prior one.

- *Discovery*. What are the *facts* about a particular college or set of colleges (including information like retention and graduation rates; postcollege experiences of alumni; the location of the school or schools; academic programs of study; admission requirements; cost and financial aid; and so forth)? Students and parents compile their early information in a variety of ways. Some of it is provided directly by colleges, like the information we provide on our websites or send to students through the mail (a still-popular way of reaching students and their parents). Other information is provided by sources neither controlled by nor even linked to the school, like guidebooks or conversations with school counselors or friends or parents. Students at this initial "discovery" stage of the admission process seek general information from which they will later narrow their choices. This stage often begins long before the student's senior year in high school and long before any institution's first formal contact with them. Much of it occurs without requiring any direct contact with a college.

- *Consideration*. What *benefits* would I receive attending this college or university (a personal look at a campus experience in the context of who I am, what I value, what I expect, and what I need)? During the consideration stage, students seek to narrow their broad set of college choices to best choices. Developing some understanding of return on investment—including intellectual investment, social investment, and financial investment—becomes a front-and-center need and expectation at this critical stage. Students and their parents want to know and understand the advantages and outcomes associated with particular institutions. Campus visits and personal interactions with staff, faculty, and students on campus, and alumni off campus, are exceedingly important during the consideration stage.

- *Selection*. Is this college or university the best *fit* for me in relation to my other choices (including my particular academic interests and expectations, my aspirations, my social needs and interests, and my family's financial situation)? Make no mistake, choosing a college ultimately is an expression of personal preference. It is not defined by a magical algorithm; as often as not, it is a decision from the heart more than the head. Students try to match their sense of self with the experiences and opportunities provided by a particular institution. It's an imperfect process, often fraught with anxiety and self-doubt (and sometimes self-deception). But colleges can and should help students make the choice that best meets the interests of the student, even if that means losing their enrollment.

At each point of the college selection process, students and their families make judgments about value through three distinct lenses:

- *Emotional value.* What kinds of emotions do I feel when I step on campus? Are there people here who are like me? Will I fit in? Will my son or daughter grow as a person here? Will she or he feel safe and nurtured? Are the school's graduates happy? Do they speak enthusiastically about their college experience here? Admissions professionals clearly understand the power of emotion in a student's choice, and the ways we deliver our marketing materials and recruitment experiences reflect it. Sensation plays a powerful role in the selection process. It matters how you and your son or daughter feel about a school.

- *Experiential value.* What opportunities will I have at this college? What academic support and guidance will I receive? What is life like in the residence halls? How do students get involved in clubs and activities? Most campus energy is focused on the experiential value we provide, largely because we understand what we own and deliver. We rightly take great pride in the curricular and cocurricular opportunities we offer. But students and families need to understand those experiences comparatively. Among the experiences that matter most to you, how does one college stand out in relation to another?

- *Economic value.* "Where can this college take me in life? What doors will the experience open after college? What kind of job will I get after graduating? What do the school's alumni do for a living? What kinds of graduate schools could I attend? Is the net price of this school in line with what we can expect by way of eventual return? Is it worth it?" Families today pay much more attention than ever to economic value and the financial return from a college education. They expect answers to their queries about return on investment. Colleges should be able to provide those answers in both emotional and numeric terms. We should be able to describe in more than superficial ways the employment experiences of our graduates, as well as the value our alumni attach to having attended our institutions.

Of course, none of this is so linear or simple as it appears. These experiences, emotions, and judgments often play out over a long period of time—and they are subject to change as your son or daughter's interests (or emotions) change and evolve. But you will experience all of them. More importantly, the whole of the process should be considered within the context of fit: students' learning who they are and how this or that college meets their needs, expectations, and aspirations.

On a campus visit with my second son, a faculty member at the college we visited declared that if the prospective students in the room had not already submitted applications for admission to ten or twelve schools, they could count themselves as behind in the process. This was mid-October, long before application deadlines. "You don't need to know where you want to go yet," the well-intentioned professor noted. "But you do need to get your name out there as far and wide as possible." I cringed. It's bad advice. The idea of scattershot followed by thoughtful consideration is unwise and simply pushes back harder thinking until later. In fact, it's not necessary to apply to ten or twelve colleges at all, and certainly not by mid-October. Although you should pay close attention to application deadlines (which are easy to find on college websites), it's better to have thought before the point of application, not after, about why you want to apply to a particular school. It will focus the process of choosing much later.

Too often students approach college admission as a landing process. Where they might go makes up the overwhelming focus of their attention, not why. Colleges also typically think that way: How many of which kinds of students will we enroll? But college is not at all a landing place. It's a launching place, a gateway experience to an aspiration beyond. As your daughter or son moves through the admission process, it's important to guide them early to think about more than the list of colleges they will generate, encouraging them to think carefully about the experiences and outcomes that matter most to them and how they will decide among the choices they have. My friend Jon Boeckenstedt is associate vice president of enrollment management at DePaul University in Chicago. He's been in the business a long time and has sent two of his own children to college. He offered me this sage advice: "Don't project your own anxiety onto your child. Avoid any articles or seminars that use words like, 'college admission craziness' or, worse, 'insanity.' If your high school senior is going to stress out, he or she doesn't need encouragement from you. Instead, do yourself a favor. Allow your child to dream, to have fun, to take time to savor the wonder of discovery." True words, indeed.

Understanding Selectivity

"Will my daughter or son get into the college they want to attend?" I get that question a lot, as does almost everyone working in or around higher education. Selectivity evokes exclusivity, making it at once a powerful object of desire and an equally powerful source of anxiety. "Should she or shouldn't she apply? Will he get accepted? How should we manage our expectations? How will they (and we) handle rejection?"

When my oldest son began to submit his applications, he asked whether he should apply to a highly selective institution we had visited on two family vacations—and where I had a number of friends and colleagues (including, as it happened, the dean of admissions). He very much liked the school, and I have no doubt he would have survived and thrived there. He was a strong and highly engaged student at his high school. His grades and test scores were good but did not rank with the highest in his class. I thought about it and ultimately advised him against applying. The profile of students attending the college made it clear that it was highly unlikely he would have been accepted for admission, and I saw no point in submitting an application for no other purpose than adding to its selectivity rate. I talked about it with my friend, the dean of admissions at the school, and he agreed with my advice. It was not an easy moment—and other parents might have chosen a different path, encouraging him to apply. But we knew enough about him and the school in advance to understand that admission likely wasn't in the cards. So he moved on, ultimately choosing a college where he has had an amazing experience. He never reduced his college experience to a search for "the one," making him wise beyond his years. He instead focused on locating a handful of institutions for which he and they were a good match. His forethought paid off. He ultimately chose a school that has served him extremely well—providing him with tremendous opportunities to learn and thrive.

Highly selective institutions receive plenty of attention. They are among the finest universities in the world and have rightly earned their "object of desire" status. The number of applications to attend those institutions has for decades vastly exceeded the number of enrollment spots available. In 2015, fewer than a dozen American colleges and universities reported acceptance rates under 10 percent. The list included Stanford University (5 percent), Harvard University (6 percent), Princeton University (7 percent), and the Massachusetts Institute of Technology (8 percent).[1] The number of applications received by those elite institutions nearly doubled between 2005 and 2015, while the number of students offered admission actually declined by 3 percent.[2] Their composite acceptance rate fell by nearly seven percentage points. In other words, they were objectively—and significantly—much harder to get into in 2015 than they were in 2005, not so much because of changing standards (they have always enrolled remarkable students) but rather because of rising demand. More people wanted to enroll there, and the spaces simply were not available.

Do those most elite institutions represent higher education generally? Unequivocally, no. In 2015–16, only one-half of one percent of all four-year institutions in the country accepted fewer than 10 percent of all students seeking admission.[3] Just 13 percent of all four-year colleges nationally offered admission to fewer than half of their applicants. More than half of all public four-year colleges and universities, and over 40 percent of all private four-year colleges, admit at least three-quarters of all students who apply. Nearly all community and technical colleges are open admission, meaning they accept nearly all students who apply. Little has changed since 2007. In total, American colleges and universities are not more exclusive or selective today than they were a decade ago.

Still, the fear of rising selectivity—and by extension exclusivity and rejection—has become a dominant narrative yielding alarming news commentary: "Rejection is more common today because the number of applicants vying for spots at colleges—big and small, attainable and out-of-reach—is soaring."[4]

It is true that the number of applications to colleges across the country has risen. Responding to a host of cues about economic opportunity, young people have flocked to college at historically high rates. Today, nearly seven in ten high school students enroll in a four-year or two-year college within one year of graduation, up from half in 1980.[5] Many colleges have experienced tremendous increases in applications for admission over just the last decade. Total enrollment has risen to meet the rising demand, but the college admission process seems crowded and even more competitive.

We need to look behind the curtain to gain some additional perspective. Aided by the Internet and easy-to-use search engines, students today have access to more information about colleges than I could ever have imagined when I went to college almost forty years ago. Search resources like Naviance (common in high school counseling offices) or the College Board's *Big Future* (https://bigfuture.collegeboard .org/) make mass amounts of information about colleges and college life readily available. No college is more than a keystroke away. Tools like the Common Application, a single, time- and effort-saving admission application form used by hundreds of colleges and universities across the country, also have made it easier to apply to more institutions at once. One form, one click, multiple applications submitted. What could be simpler? In the fall of 2016, nearly 60 percent of all first-time new students enrolling at four-year colleges and universities in the United States applied for admission to at least five schools, up from 37 percent in the fall of 2000 and just 26 percent in the fall of 1990.[6]

As any economist would tell you, however, demand is a tricky, often illusory thing to measure. The trend of rising applications has not resulted principally from more students competing to get into college. The number of high school graduates in the country leveled off by 2014 and will not begin to grow again until the middle of the 2020s (and then only for a brief time).[7] Instead, it mostly reflects students applying to more colleges.

But no matter how many colleges a student applies to, they can choose only one, which has had the somewhat ironic or counterintuitive effect of making enrollment goals at many schools less certain even as the number of applications they receive has risen. What feels like a seller's market is, for most colleges and universities, actually a buyer's market. Students and families have far more market power than they did even a decade ago. In a fall 2016 survey conducted by the online journal, *Inside Higher Education*, nearly two-thirds of all public and private college admissions deans and directors surveyed reported that they had not met their new student enrollment goal.[8] No matter how a college projects its selectivity, if it cannot attain its enrollment goal, selectivity becomes irrelevant.

When talking to high school students and their parents, I often have wondered how they determined where to apply to college, particularly when their lists include schools that appear completely different in terms of size, location, experience, selectivity, or mission. I suspect the answer lies not so much in the broadening interests of students but rather with the changing ways and means that colleges approach them as they shape and consider their options. We send out more mail than ever designed to entice the interest of more students than ever. We have fully utilized the Internet and social media to reach more students and simplify the application process. It has worked. Students have responded to our invitation beyond what anyone could have imagined twenty or even ten years ago.

But more may not always mean better. As students have added more colleges to their lists for consideration—the admissions equivalent of speed dating—they may have increased the difficulty of settling on a comfortable final choice. The percentage of students nationally who report landing at their first-choice school has fallen as the number of colleges to which they apply has increased. In the fall of 1990, when one-quarter of all new four-year college students applied to just one institution, seven in ten reported that that they had enrolled at their first (and often only) choice. By 2015, when 58 percent applied to five or more schools, fewer than six in ten described the college they chose as their first choice.[9] At my institutions, our new students who apply to five or more colleges are more than twenty percentage points less likely than their classmates who apply to four or fewer schools to cite us as their first-choice school. Rather than expanding opportunity, it may well be that for some students, more options have led to less clarity about their final choice. The issue is not simply the number of colleges to which a student applies, but rather the time needed to consider choices and set expectations. It has never been easier to apply to college—and it likely will get easier as colleges seek even more applicants. However, the relative ease of application does not replace the need to think carefully about the choice.

According to the National Association for College Admission Counseling (NACAC), the aggregate acceptance rate across all four-year colleges in the United States in 2014 was nearly 65 percent, only slightly lower than it was in 2003.[10] That statistic has great meaning to colleges, which often use it to evaluate their place in the pecking order of higher education. However, it conveys little useful information to students and parents. For any given student, the actual acceptance rate likely is 100 percent: there is a college in America somewhere, likely even close to home, that will accept the student and at which they can have a tremendous experience. It may not be a student's first choice, nor even among the colleges on their initial "dream" list. But it may well be a school that provides them with an extraordinary education. Selectivity has only ever indicated how many get in. It does not describe fit or value for any specific student. That is up to you to discover.

It's a mistake to approach the college admission process as an almost romantic endeavor to find "the one"—the very best and only place for your daughter or son. It's a nice thought, though somewhat quixotic. Reality suggests that most students could succeed at many, many institutions, despite their selectivity or reputation. But how many schools should a student consider? The search tools available today to explore colleges are remarkable, meaning our kids can actively consider more schools than ever. They should consider many schools. Read the materials, visit the websites, talk to the college representatives at schools or college fairs, visit the campuses if you get a chance. But that doesn't mean you should apply to every school you see and like. I've never been a fan of applications that are played like a collection of baseball cards (a throwback reference to the days of my youth when we bought and traded baseball player cards as prizes). Use the discovery process to look far and wide, and use the consideration process that follows to narrow the choices. I typically recommend that students apply to no more than four to six institutions—and I always recommend that they apply to at least two so they can form a comparison (even if they have discovered "the one"). At least one school to which they apply should be a stretch—an institution where admission is possible but not guaranteed. The others should be colleges at which a student not only is likely to be accepted but also where she or he can thrive. I intensely dislike the term *safety school*—a pejorative phrase meant to diminish both an institution and the student. A school that is a good match is never a safety school.

A final word about selectivity. Parents often ask me how colleges could say no to their son or daughter—a student who seemed so accomplished. Indignation follows. What were they thinking? The simple answer is that at highly selective institutions, and even those that are somewhat less selective, it's impossible to forecast who gets in and who is left out. Those choices are a function of the characteristics of students who make up the applicant pool in any particular year and the needs and interests of the college in putting its class together. Highly selective institutions may not admit a student with a perfect SAT score but instead may admit someone who is an exceptional student but also an accomplished first violinist. They try to balance academic achievement with, among other things, geographic diversity, extracurricular achievement and involvement, and personal and academic promise. The characteristics of the admission pool at all colleges, from the most selective to the least, by definition change and vary each year as an entirely new group of students seek admission. The selection process is holistic—meaning schools look at much more than grades and test scores. Applications and reference letters typically are read multiple times by admission staff and often faculty committees and even alumni readers, making the process nearly impossible to subject to either an easy-to-understand algorithm or speculative guessing.

It may well be that your daughter or son will experience the disappointment of a "no" on an application for admission. It may be the first time they have experienced academic disappointment or rejection of any kind. You may feel that disappointment for yourself, as well. But an admission decision, positive or negative, is neither a referendum on everything your son or daughter is or can be nor a judgment about the quality of your parenting. Rather it's a moment from which we, as parents, and they need to move on, beyond the illusion of "the one." As parents, we need to see beyond our child's disappointment, console, and move on. Remarkable experiences await.

The Visit

"Mom, you cannot say anything while we tour. And you absolutely cannot tell them what you do or who you are." So said the daughter of a colleague to her mother as they began their college visits. Her mother happened to be a college president.

I learned my own ground rules quickly on the first college tour I took with my oldest son. Up to that point, he had mostly asked me whether this or that college was a "good school," a question I chose always to answer with another question: "What are you looking for?" (a response he consistently found annoying and unsatisfying). The tour represented our first attempt to learn something about the college up close and personal. I likely was more excited about the visit than he was (it was, after all, my first college tour as a parent), but I had decided beforehand that I would simply listen, playing—appropriately— the role of father, not college professional. I knew it was important to really see what my son was seeing and hear what he was hearing so we could talk about it later. I had grand plans to ask him afterward to write down the pluses and minuses he saw and then discuss them over coffee. We would have a textbook father-son moment. Cue the music.

It didn't quite play out that way. During the admission presentation, my son looked at me every time the college representative cited a number—as if I was an authority on the college's data (I wasn't). But when I took the one moment I had to actually ask a question, about the college's general education curriculum, he quickly swung his head and gave me a look that combined terror and death: "Please don't embarrass me." That ended the oral part of my tour exam. I stayed mostly quiet the rest of the tour, save for occasional harmless (meaning, not-embarrassing-to-my-son) banter with the tour guide. My recommendation about my son's writing a summary of the tour did not go as planned, either. Though I was certain he had enjoyed the experience and learned a lot, the most cogent response I received at the close of the visit was, "Yeah, I really liked it. It's a good school." Welcome to the conversational world of the 18-year-old boy.

Campus visits are among the most important parts of the college admission process. They offer the best opportunity to experience a school in real time, to meet personally with students and faculty, and to understand the rhythms of a day in the life of a college. Each summer, my office surveys newly admitted and enrolled students. Among other things, we ask them which sources of information or which experiences were most useful at the time they began their college search. Year in and year out, campus visits rank first; more than eight in ten newly admitted and enrolled students describe their campus visit as "very useful." No other information source comes close. Parents rank second as an information source, with nearly six in ten students describing information from their family as very useful (meaning we actually do have an important role to play as sages). Interestingly, our new students were more than twice as likely to describe campus visits as very useful, compared to college websites. In spite of websites' ubiquity and ease of access, fewer than half of our new students described them as most useful at the beginning of their college search. Tangible experience, where students can see, smell, hear, taste, and touch, outdo the virtual or vicarious.

I always advise parents to participate in campus visits with their sons and daughters if they have the opportunity. It's best to go, if possible, when school is actually in session and the campus is abuzz with activity. The visit affords parents an opportunity to experience what their children experience and serves as a base for a later conversation. Even though my own children have not yet been particularly interested in the questions I have asked during tours (apparently deeming the risk of public humiliation too great), they have always asked questions later, after the tours were over. Participating in the visit, even as a silent partner, makes it far easier to talk about pros and cons later and to explore the nature of the fit. Everyone begins the conversation on the same page.

Tour guides play a crucial role in the selection process because in many ways they must represent all of the college's students. I'm certain my own children have assessed the various tour guides they've encountered by whether they could imagine them as friends. Student guides, sometimes called ambassadors, are not randomly chosen. In fact, colleges want them to represent the larger student body. Professional staff in the admission office train them, of course, to provide prospective students and their families with relevant and, hopefully, accurate information. But no admission office commands complete control of their student tour guides (nor should they)—and the guides often provide the most unvarnished view of the college and campus life. Be prepared to ask your guides questions about why they chose the college, the activities they are involved in, and how a typical day on campus plays out. You'll learn a lot, often about experiences not included in glossy admission publications.

You may wonder what the appropriate parental etiquette is on a tour. I have participated on campus tours both as a parent and as an observer. Families comport themselves in a variety of different ways. Some parents do all the talking, essentially assigning their children observer status. Others follow quietly, saying little or nothing along the way. Neither is exactly right or wrong, though I offer four recommendations in advance of a family campus visit:

- Keep in mind that it is your daughter or son's experience, not yours. I find it fascinating when parents begin a question about the college experience with the pronoun "we": "We are looking for a college with exceptional study abroad experiences. We want a college with a strong internship program," and so on. Parents have a legitimate interest in the collegiate experiences their sons and daughters will have. Still, it is more productive to encourage your children to ask those kinds of questions on their own behalf, providing them an opportunity to express their own voice, values, and expectations.

- Define in advance the questions you most need answered during your visit. Those questions often involve the cost of college and financial aid. They may involve other accommodations your child requires, such as support for a learning or physical disability. Take the time to ask those questions either with or without your child present. Not asking a question important to you represents an opportunity lost.

- Learn something about the college before the visit—and insist that your daughter or son do likewise. Given the importance of the visit and tour, it's worth taking some time to understand the school in advance. What programs does it offer? What kinds of experiences and outcomes does it describe in its materials? What does it cost? The more you and your child know in advance, the better the questions you will ask, and the better the visit will become as a means for later making a choice.

- Sit down with your daughter or son before the tour so you can talk about your mutual expectations for the visit. The classic horror story goes something like this: you've driven hundreds of miles from home to a college, and as you drive onto campus, your suddenly focused child announces that they already know that this school won't work for them, requiring an immediate and awkward recalibration of expectations. Your visit will go much better for you and your daughter or son if you've done your homework in advance, identified questions important to each of you, and shared your expectations of each other for the visit.

All colleges understand the influence of visits on the college choice. Students who visit campus, particularly if they do so multiple times, are much more likely to enroll than those who do not. That's why admission offices work so hard to prepare and stage visit days. The stakes are high for college and student alike. However, we also know that not everyone will have an opportunity to make a campus visit, particularly if the visit requires long-distance travel.

Fortunately, you need not rule out a college from consideration if you are not able to visit. Many schools offer very good online virtual tours, complete with student interviews, which provide both an informational and sensory experience of campus. Most host admission chat rooms, providing prospective students with an opportunity to talk directly with college students and sometimes even with other prospective students. Many schools hold admitted-student nights across the country, an attempt to bring the college to students and to connect them to alumni and other prospective students. Beyond the admission process, most colleges and universities live-stream concerts, lectures, or athletic events—each a significant opportunity to learn something about the school. The bottom line is that there are more ways to "visit" a campus today than ever before. It pays to take advantage of those opportunities.

Campus visits—real or virtual—provide opportunities for an immediate and sensory assessment of a college. It's like looking behind the marketing curtain. Does the college act out or show as it is described and depicted in its marketing materials? More than just a stroll through leafy walkways, academic buildings, and residence halls, the visit also creates opportunities to see and feel what life is like beyond the borders of campus. Particularly at residential colleges, where the school becomes home, the setting and neighborhoods around the campus are as important as the campus itself. Treat the campus visit seriously. You'll know more at the end of those visits than you could ever learn from publications, guide books, or college fairs.

Stats

In an era of "big data," it's now easier than ever to gather and analyze an enormous variety of statistics about colleges. I've spent much of my professional life creating and devouring those statistics, which I find both useful and fascinating. My children find it nerdy. The data fill guidebooks, websites, and college marketing materials. You can easily access information now on everything from endowment size to spending per student to average faculty salaries to number of admission applications to number of staff, and lots in between. A world of data exists with only a few keyboard strokes. But it's also easier than ever to feel overwhelmed by the data dump, particularly when numbers that appear similar or similarly collected may, in fact, be different in important but nuanced (and unclear) ways. You shouldn't need a degree in research methods and analysis to understand something important about a school.

Not all college statistics are of equal value—and few of them convey anything about the lived college experience. Still, from the vantage point of students and families engaged in a college search, some data are more important than others, though the important and less important often are lumped together in a kind of numeric mosh pit. You will need to determine for yourself and your family which statistics matter the most to you. But there are some broad data worthy of particular attention. Five come immediately to mind:

- *Class size*. This is not to be confused with the popular student-to-faculty ratio, a contrived statistic important to college planning and budgeting but utterly opaque to students and families. Average and median class size describe the kind of experience a student may actually have in a classroom and the kind of individual attention they might receive. In addition to the average, it's also valuable to ask about the upper limits of class size. Which classes are largest and how are they taught?

- *Retention rates.* How many students who enroll at the institution as new students return in subsequent years? Students leave school before completion for a variety of reasons, sometimes related to money but just as often related to academic, social, or personal issues and challenges. High retention rates typically signal two things: the students at the school are satisfied and committed enough to return year after year, and the school has systems in place to ensure that students get the academic, financial, and personal support they need to return.

- *Completion rates.* How many students who start at the college earn their degree there, and how long does it take? National data sources these days typically report six-year completion rates (though they still describe undergraduate colleges as four-year colleges, an odd mismatch). Both four-year and six-year completion rates are useful. They measure the percentage of an entering class's students who stay to earn their degrees. In statistical parlance, the completion rate could be described as a "survivor rate." Most students who enroll in college expect to eventually earn a degree, and the primary economic value and return associated with a college education rests with degree completion. Like retention rates, high completion rates can be interpreted as signs of both a successful college and a successful collegiate experience.

  Colleges also often report time to completion. Easily confused with completion rates, time to completion measures the time it takes students to earn their degrees. Whereas completion evaluates student movement from start to finish, time to completion starts on the other end and asks, "Of those who earned degrees, how long did it take?" A college can report a low completion rate (the product of many students leaving prior to graduating) but rapid time to completion of those who stayed (for example, 90 percent of those who stayed earn their degree in four years or less). Longer times to completion come with an economic price, in the form of additional years of college costs and the opportunity cost of lost earnings.

- *First destination summaries.* Though not a phrase commonly used outside of a collegiate setting, the term "first destination" describes what happens to students shortly after graduation. In days gone by, this would have been labeled the school's placement rate—a term that no longer accurately describes the range of outcomes students might experience. First destination summaries indicate how many students find jobs, enroll in graduate school, or commit to full-time volunteer positions within six months or one year of graduating. Though the summaries represent only the most immediate returns to college (keep in mind that the typical work life now spans forty-five years, an unimaginably long time through the eyes of an 18- or 22-year-old), first destination results are of keen interest to parents. Do most of this college's graduates find a suitable landing place for themselves? In other words, do they launch successfully? Some colleges, my own included, post complete student-by-student databases online (names not included, of course) that allow prospective students to examine and sort first destination by major, location, employer, and type of activity. Ask about response rates: What percentage of a college's graduates actually supplied first destination information? More is always preferable to less.

- *Alumni satisfaction.* How do alumni evaluate their experience at the college? If they could start college over (a wistful thought, to be sure), would they make the same choice? Would they choose the same major again? Some colleges gather this data, others don't. All should. I prefer to collect data from younger alumni, who have a contemporary and still fresh understanding of their college experience and its value. Alumni represent past buyers. Their satisfaction (or not) speaks volumes about an institution.

Though hardly comprehensive, these five data points are commonly collected and broadly comparable among institutions. They collectively provide a useful starting point for you and your daughter or son to evaluate the experience at a particular college.

Fear of Choice

"What if I make a bad choice?" Many students and parents ask, or at least think about, that question. For some, a bad roommate experience describes a bad choice. For others, it's a poor classroom experience or a bad academic advising encounter or discomfort with the campus

TO PARENTS OF FIRST-GENERATION COLLEGE STUDENTS

For families with no history of college attendance, the admission process can be both daunting and mysterious. Beyond alphabet acronyms and the twists and turns of a lengthy and often labyrinthine process lies a hidden curriculum of assumptions that favor those with prior experience. Colleges make many assumptions about the academic and social skills students require to succeed on campus. College professionals assume them because they have developed over years or decades and are now simply a part of the way we operate, unspoken and generally well understood (or so we think). We mostly assume that prospective students understand that it is in their best interests to take rigorous courses (like AP courses) and college entrance exams (like the SAT or ACT). We assume prospective students will act in their own best interest to seek and find the colleges that work best for them. Once enrolled, we assume new students will, eventually, sort out the processes that drive course choices, social choices, and the day-to-day choices that shape their college experience. And it works, for most students. But it can be remarkably difficult and foreign to those for whom the experience of college is new.

Fortunately, today colleges and universities of all types recognize the limits of their assumptions. We have created programs to meet the needs of students for whom college is a new family experience—helping them to break through the assumptions and providing them with the support and guidance they need to succeed. Jillian Hiscock works for College Possible, a national nonprofit organization committed to college access and success for low-income students.* She is among the most passionate advocates I know, deeply committed to educational opportunity. She offers direct advice for parents of first-generation college students:

> Too often in higher education, it is assumed that students and their families have extensive knowledge about the inner workings of the confusing systems and processes on college campuses. As a parent

---

*College Possible is an extraordinary organization, founded in Minneapolis in 2000 and now serving students across the country. It is one of many community-based organizations around the country dedicated to success and opportunity for underrepresented, low-income, and first-generation students. The organization does remarkable work expanding opportunities for students. You can learn more about College Possible at http://www.collegepossible.org/about/.

(continued)

of a first-generation college student, one of the most beneficial skills you can encourage in your child is the confidence to ask questions. The most successful students I work with are comfortable asking questions and knowing when to seek out the help of others. Encouraging them to ask questions will plant an important seed in their development as lifelong learners. It is possible to teach the skills that ultimately lead to self-advocacy by nurturing a child's curiosity and confidence when they are young.

Hiscock's advice actually works for all students and families but is especially valuable to those for whom college is new.

social scene. But all of those experiences could happen at any school, even the most highly selective. Unlike the purchase of a retail good, it's nearly impossible to know the particulars of a college experience—either in terms of what it will be like on campus or what happens after graduation—until it is experienced.

The basic college experience consists of two independent but interacting parts, one uniquely owned by students, the other by colleges and universities themselves. As I explained earlier, all students bring three things to the table when they enroll in college: their aptitude, their motivation, and their aspirations. They own those values and attributes. Each is shaped in a variety of ways long before a student ever shows up on campus or in a classroom. Aptitude, motivation, and aspiration all are influenced by the environments in which students live and grow up—in their families, in their schools, with their friends, and in the broader culture. Colleges can influence but never own all three. That's an important point. On the one hand, colleges take students as they come, each one a unique bundle of values and characteristics. On the other hand, students' values and attributes act on colleges, shaping and reshaping institutional values and practices.

Colleges and universities also bring three distinct features to the educational table: our purpose (embodied in our mission and values), our product (the constellation of courses and experiences we provide to our students), and our processes (the ways we deliver those experiences). Together, those values and attributes represent not only what we offer to individual students but also what we pledge to society at large. Like the values and attributes of our students, our institutional purposes, products, and processes are drawn from our history, our values, and our interpretation of the changing needs and demands of the world around us. Because these typically have been shaped over many decades, we often hold them very dear—resisting the temptation to faddish change, and sometimes to any change at all.

The successful fulfillment of a students' aspirations requires the student's full commitment and effort. Students do not simply receive their education, they give it form and define its outcomes. This is true at every level of schooling and at every kind of college. A course can be magnificently constructed and brilliantly presented, but without the active engagement of the student's aptitude, motivation, and aspiration, little learning or development will occur. The bargain, of course, works in reverse. Bright, fully engaged students get little out of college experiences that are poorly constructed or poorly presented. In either case, no input yields no outcome. By definition and necessity, education is an interactive process, an exchange—colleges and their students acting on each other. Students themselves are the primary input to their own outcome. Good and bad are not defined by guidebooks, or websites, or rankings, or statistical profiles. They are defined by the unique interactions of a student with the experiences a college provides.

The engagement of a student's aptitude, motivation, and aspirations with an institution's purpose, product, and processes constitutes the touchstone of the collegiate experience. When those values and attributes are reasonably well aligned (what I would describe as a good fit), the educational experience yields marvelous results: engaged students who resonate with the values of a college and take full advantage of the range of learning opportunities it provides to create powerful professional and developmental outcomes. A happy ending for everyone. When they are not well aligned, it is a different and more difficult and complicated story.

As I have noted throughout, the only bad college choice is an unconsidered or not fully considered choice. Students need to take the time to reflect on their own aptitude, motivation, and aspirations in the context of the experiences and values of the colleges they consider. There are myriad ways students can have an amazing college experience anywhere they choose to enroll. There also are myriad ways they can have a difficult experience. There are no a priori guarantees in either direction, but students can push the needle toward success and fulfillment by thinking in advance about who they are and what they expect in relation to what a college or university offers or does. Happy endings, and they are common, are not the product of fate or an invisible hand. They result when both parties—the student and the college— are on the same page. When that happens, anything is possible. Oh, the places they'll go!

Senioritis

The senior year of high school is more complex, and more important, than it seems. Often overwhelmed by the college search or the sense of transition from one thing to another, childhood to adulthood, many students are tempted to check out of school or to simply coast through the year. "My applications are complete. I've submitted my grades and test scores. I lined up my recommendations. Now I just have to wait. I'm done and now I can sit back, relax, and enjoy the year." My own children offered various versions of that familiar refrain. It rightfully drives high school teachers and counselors crazy.

Make no mistake: coasting through the senior year as if it didn't matter is a bad choice. All colleges and universities require final high school transcripts. Significant changes in academic performance in the senior year can influence academic scholarships and, in rare cases, even the offer of admission. More than that, though, it's important that students continue to work hard and develop as learners all the way to the high school finish line. That commitment, and those learning skills, will serve them well in college. The first semester of college often is a shocking experience academically. The pace and quantity of academic work, as well as higher academic expectations, can test even the best prepared students. We find at the colleges I work at that new students who say they did little academically during their senior year (meaning they spent little time outside of class studying or preparing for class) often struggle the most during their first year of college, irrespective of their high school grade point average or test scores. Simply put, it is difficult to go from zero to sixty or to flip a switch on demand. Though it may not seem like it to our children, and they may not like to hear it, in the end it is easier for them to maintain their commitment to learning throughout their senior year than it is to slack off and try to recharge the next year.

May Day

The National Association for College Admission Counseling defines May 1 as the "National Candidates Reply Date," the deadline for students to accept an admission offer and make a tuition deposit at their college of choice. As part of their Statement of Principles of Good Practice, all postsecondary members of NACAC agree to "permit first-year candidates for fall admission to choose among offers of admission and institutionally-affiliated financial aid and scholarships until May 1, and state this deadline explicitly in their offers of admission."[11] The vast majority of colleges and universities in the United States are members of NACAC and commit to the association's principles of good practice and code of ethics. The May 1 reply date provides students with the time to fully consider their offers of admission and financial aid to make the best collegiate choice they can. It explicitly forbids colleges from seeking to manipulate students to commit themselves earlier. It's an important practice. Students can make their enrollment choice at any time after they have received an offer of admission, but no institution can compel the choice before May 1. Even after May 1, when, if they choose, colleges can ethically rescind an unaccepted offer of admission, most don't. Nearly all students make their choice by the time summer begins, providing them valuable time to prepare for the transition from high school to college.

Although it may be tempting to encourage your daughter or son to select a college sooner rather than later, it's important that they take the time they need to consider and make their choice. That said, you can help and encourage them not to simply put it off. Ideally, they will use the time before May 1 to reflect on fit, their aspirations and preferences, and their expectations. May 1 seems a far-off date when seen from the November before, when students begin to submit their college applications. But as with so many other things in life, the time quickly goes by.

Having extended an offer of admission, colleges and universities across the country typically use predictive models to gauge the probability of a student's eventual enrollment. Just as students waited for a "yes" from a college, so too do colleges wait for a "yes" from students. Though the models vary from school to school, all predictive models examine both student characteristics and a student's expression of interest (which includes contact with admissions office representatives and campus visits, among other things) to assess the likelihood of their eventual enrollment. The formulas are mathematical, elegant in their own way—and wildly imperfect. Sophisticated though the models and algorithms may be, what we don't know about how a student weighs a choice almost always outweighs what we do know. Try as we might, most of the time we are not able to get into the heads of prospective students to really understand what they are thinking and what they value. Which should sound familiar to any parent of a teenager.

Two lessons from years ago made this exceptionally clear to me. One of our senior admissions representatives described the choices of two students, one of whom we enrolled, the other who enrolled elsewhere. As the May 1 admission reply date approached, the first student described himself as unable to decide between us and another university. As he wrestled with his choices to no apparent avail, he noticed that the deposit reply form from Saint John's University sat on top of the kitchen table (hearkening back to the time when colleges sweated out the daily mail, rather than daily email). He told us that the envelope on the table was a "sign" that fate had intervened and called him to enroll at Saint John's. It's a nice story (for us, at least), but I know that we have no variable for "fate" in any of our predictive models. The second student found himself in a similar quandary, unable to make his enrollment choice at the deadline. However, rather than relying on fate, he turned to a higher power—his mother—and asked her to choose for him. She preferred that he live nearby and so chose a college close to home. We definitely have no variable for "mom's choice" in any of our predictive models. Nor do we have variables for "the food was good," "it rained," or "it just felt right." But all of them matter. Any college could tell similar stories. Try as we might on campus to reduce the college decision to a clear rational choice, emotion and all of its vagaries often win out.

Each fall, I survey our first-year students and their parents. Separately. We learn a lot about why they choose us and what they valued most during their college search. It's clear that parents and students value many characteristics and experiences differently, which isn't particularly surprising. We also ask who made the enrollment decision. We provide three choices for answers: the choice was entirely the student's, the choice was a joint decision of student and parents, or parents made the choice for the student. Year in and year out, two-thirds of our students describe the choice as entirely their own. But, year in and year out, nearly two-thirds of their parents describe the decision as a joint family effort. Almost no one—student or parent—confesses to the third choice. It's gratifying that so many of our new students describe the choice as entirely their own. It suggests confidence. But I'm equally impressed with the parent responses. We know that parents play an important role throughout the admission process, but in the end they say that they provide the space for their daughters and sons to make their choice. And that's the ultimate lesson. No matter what role you play during your son or daughter's college search, they need to own their own choice. It can be tricky—guiding over cajoling, empowering over usurping, managing fear and anxiety rather than shielding them from it. But as your children will live their collegiate experience, so they should be empowered to choose it.

SIX

A New Chapter

You do not need to know precisely what is happening, or exactly where it is all going. What you need is to recognize the possibilities and challenges offered by the present moment, and to embrace them with courage, faith and hope.
—Thomas Merton

✉ From Betsy Johnson-Miller, Assistant Professor of English, College of Saint Benedict and Saint John's University, and Shane Miller, Professor of Communication, College of Saint Benedict and Saint John's University, Minnesota

Dear Parents,

One of us secretly thinks that a great perk of having kids is that you can play video games again (with them, of course) and not look pathetic. Many of the students we teach also game. A lot. What does this have to do with helping your kids through college? We often refer to the students at our college as young adults. And they are. But perhaps another helpful way of thinking of them is as people who are experimenting with adulthood for the first time. They are new adults, with new boundaries and expectations, demands and opportunities. They are, in the language of gaming, beta testing adulthood.

"Beta testing" refers to the process whereby a new game (or program or app) is developed to a point where it works and can be tested by users. The basic structure of the game is in place but needs to be subjected to real-world conditions. The program's developers cannot know what to change until the testing is done. They use the experiences of real gamers to figure out what works and what doesn't, what can be kept, what can be dropped, and what can be improved.

This can be a helpful way of thinking about college—a time when your child is beta testing their first step into adulthood. It's hard. We get that. They may be living away from their home and family in a new space filled with new people. They are transitioning into classrooms with higher expectations and demands on their time and work. On top of that, you also may be paying a tremendous amount of money to provide them with this opportunity. Of course you want them to succeed, and of course you want to do anything you can to help them. But that is where it gets tricky. What kind of help? How much? When should you help, and when should you back off? If we use beta testing as a guide, the answer to these questions lies in the development of your child. What skills or attitudes or values do you want them to develop for adulthood?

Self-reliance? Then when they call you, frustrated with a grade or a professor, ask yourself what kind of response from you will help them to be more self-reliant.

Dealing with complexity or ambiguity? When your child complains that they don't understand an assignment or lab results, what advice can you give to help them find the answers they need, or identify the situations where there are no easy or certain answers?

Learning to handle failure? When the paper they've worked on for weeks comes back with a low grade, or after dozens of hours of code-writing and debugging, their computer program still doesn't work, what can you do to help them persevere?

This sounds obvious—easy, even—in theory. In practice it's much more difficult. When our children struggle, we naturally want to fix the problem. It's what we've done for years. However, if we want our children to become functioning and adept adults, letting them figure it out for themselves might be better.

We experienced this with our daughter. During her first year at college, we watched her change from a bubbly and self-assured young woman into someone who was sad, withdrawn, and uncertain.

It became obvious to us that the college she was attending was not a good fit. However, we knew it was vital that she come to that conclusion on her own. So instead of saying, "You need to transfer," we listened to her struggles and asked questions to help her figure out what wasn't working. It turned out that she couldn't "find her people" at the school she chose, nor did she like living in the big city where it was located. Had we swooped in and fixed it for her—simply telling her what she should do—she might not have gained the valuable awareness of who she was and what she wanted out of college and out of life. We did not want our daughter to be a passive observer in her own life, watching us play the game for her. In due course, she concluded on her own that she should transfer to a school that better fit her personality and needs. A happy new beginning, and a lesson in resilience.

Difficult though it may be to follow at times, our best advice is to let your child test and adjust and learn in these, and other, situations. Picking up the phone or shooting off an email on their behalf may make you feel better, but it most definitely will not help your child master the game that is adulthood.

 From Jody Terhaar, Dean of Students, College of Saint Benedict, Minnesota

Dear Parents,

You may be familiar with stories about "helicopter parents," those moms and dads deeply—and overly—involved in every aspect of the lives of their children. As dean of students at a small college, I have collected many stories about parents who inserted themselves into their child's college experience. These include the parent who wanted to live with their student for the first two weeks of the semester "just to make sure she was getting settled in and making friends"; and the parent who asked who would wake her daughter each morning because she had never done that on her own. I have interacted with good, caring parents who begin their calls or emails to me with the assertion or apology, "I don't want to be a helicopter parent, but . . ." I can hear the chopper blades in the background when I receive those calls.

I'm not just a dean of students. I also am a parent of a college grad-uate, a current college student, and a college student yet to be. Like you, I want my children to grow into adults with meaningful lives and healthy relationships. I have had to let go of my wants and needs, my ego, and my sense of who I am as a parent because at times what has been best for my child is to let them fail, struggle, and experience dis-comfort. I have fought against my desire to "fix things" with a phone call, money, or by just taking care of it myself. I have had to suppress a bit of worry that my child's mistakes, irresponsibility, or unhappiness may be seen as a reflection of my own parenting.

As a dean of students and fellow parent, I offer the following advice for parenting your college student:

- Build capacity in your daughter or son to take ownership and responsibility for their experiences and to learn from mistakes and disappointment. Challenge them to consider their own actions, decisions, and behaviors when something doesn't go well rather than simply letting them place responsibility on other people or circumstances seemingly out of their own control. Help them to identify steps they can take, as well as the resources and people who can provide guidance and support, to help them resolve situa-tions like roommate conflict (very common), poor grades, a college conduct policy violation, or not being selected for a leadership position. Avoid the temptation to solve problems for your children and instead help them learn to find solutions to problems they will encounter.

- Help your son or daughter appreciate the experience of being uncomfortable and the opportunity discomfort provides for growth and self-awareness. Your student will encounter different ideas, people from other backgrounds, and concepts that challenge them to consider "truths" different from those they hold. Encourage them to interact with people different from themselves, to consider other points of view, and to seek out a wide variety of experiences and perspectives throughout their college career.

- Talk with your daughter or son about what it means to respect themselves and others. College is a time when many students test boundaries, explore relationships, and try new things. These conversations can be difficult and possibly embarrassing, but they are important. Talk with your student about situations they may encounter and decisions they may face about alcohol use, sexual activity, social media, friends, and academics. I never cease to be amazed at the level of intelligence, curiosity, and compassion that I encounter in students. I also am as frequently dismayed at how callous, petty, and reckless these same students can be toward each other. Talk with your student about the kind of person they want to be and the decisions and behaviors that reflect that ideal. Revisit the conversations often by asking open-ended questions and listening to what they have to share. Although you may hear things that cause you to cringe or make you want to yell, "What were you thinking!?," these conversations can become a safe space to talk about experiences and mistakes and to help them develop better decision-making abilities.

Sending a child to college is not about "letting go" or no longer being a parent. Rather, it is a time to explore and nurture a maturing relationship with your child as they enter full adulthood. Your role will change, but the relationship and its importance will endure.

✉ **From Carol Bruess, Professor of Communication and Journalism and Director of Family Studies at the University of St. Thomas, Minnesota, and Brian Bruess, President, St. Norbert College, Wisconsin**

Dear Parents,

You may be receiving much the same advice we did: "Ya gotta just let go!" or, "You don't have to let go; just let them grow." Or multiple versions of, "Don't be a helicopter parent, hovering and paving the way." We actually don't have much advice for you, although what we can share is our rather mundane little story. We hope you will find embedded in it something useful for your own journey and transition.

It was September 2014. As we packed and then hauled the three slightly-over-the-airline-weight-limit bags and boarded the plane in Minneapolis with our son, the only thing we knew for sure was that we needed to embrace what we, as academics ourselves, knew best: that our job at this stage of our son's life was simply to continue to be his parents, to continue teaching and guiding him. The form and intensity of that teaching would, of course, need to take slightly new shape, one that for at least one of us (the mother of this parenting pair) took a few months to iron out. What we can perhaps offer you, based on our launch experience, is that all of us as parents must remember that we are forever parents and teachers, even as we gently or happily or begrudgingly or tentatively push our children out of the nest. The most effective parenting is always and forever best practiced by keeping the developmentally appropriate needs of our children front and center.

With that in mind, we share with you the only thing we could think best for us to do in the weeks leading up to pushing our son from our cozy nest. We wrote him a letter and slipped it to him just days before we headed west. Our goal? To articulate our continued dreams and hopes for him as he entered this exciting, next life chapter. We allowed ourselves the fantasy that he would find the letter in his desk on a random day when he needed it most! The theme of our letter: "Becoming."

As you find your way to college and beyond, we know you are becoming an even wiser and more whole version of your already-perfect self.

- *As you become a scholar*, remember the perpetual value of a liberal education. Deep wisdom comes from listening, reflecting, and wondering. Critical thinking, analytical perspective, and perpetual justice shall rule the day. A great student you already are and a fine scholar you will continue to become.

- *As you become a brother*, continue to do as you always have: offering your watchful eye and loyal encouragement to that sister of yours. Each smile, each bit of joy and laughter, each kind word and faithful praise you offer is something we have always admired—each the gift of precious siblinghood. She has been blessed by your respect and love and been lifted by your role modeling. She will continue to watch you, and for that we are grateful.

- *As you become a son*, about whom we will continue to worry, be your best self and remember that regardless of how independent you become, know you are never alone. You grace us with natural cause for big joy, the magnitude of which no mother or father could have ever imagined. As you become an older son, know that we are forever your greatest fans and source of unconditional love.

- *As you become a friend*, lean on your generous, gentle, and expansive heart. Radical love of every human has always been your way. Continue to prioritize authentic friendship, the likes of which can never be substituted.

- *As you become a citizen*, give generously—always a bit more than you think you can. Be kinder than you think you need to be. May every person you meet know your regard, love, and care for social justice. May your professional success be outshone only by your personal sacrifice for the good of others.

- *As you become a whole person*, nourish your entire self: the emotional, spiritual, intellectual, social, and physical. May gentle consideration and moderation always be your center. As you struggle to find and retain equilibrium, treat your full self—as you do others—with dignity, kindness, and love.

As you continue to grow and become, know that you could not be cheered on and supported with a more profound love than that which we, your parents, send quietly and confidently with you on this journey. Go forth, dear child. Be fully you. And, as you can be honest with that self, we have zero doubt you will be your best self in this beautiful world.

With unspeakable love,
Mom and Dad

Move-In Day

One of the great privileges of working on a college campus is the opportunity to experience move-in day. Families arrive with carloads and vanloads of clothing, shoes, televisions, computers, futons, bean bag chairs, bedding, gaming equipment, microwaves, refrigerators, fans, bicycles, area rugs, occasionally books, pictures, knickknacks, and mementos. And more. For Target, Amazon, and Walmart, move-in day is like Black Friday.

A standard dorm room for two students typically does not measure more than twelve feet by sixteen feet. It may or may not include a sink. The electrical power requirements of a contemporary dorm room now likely exceed the power required to send astronauts to the moon in 1969. I recall fitting nearly everything I owned comfortably into the back of our station wagon, with plenty of room remaining for seating. In the stone ages. The days of ascetic college living have long passed. Yet, although the sheer mass of student gear has increased nearly exponentially, what hasn't changed is the sense of home that quickly develops once students have moved in. Though the dorm room has a stuffed-phone-booth quality (a cultural reference nearly no new student today would understand), it's amazing how quickly the contents of the packing boxes and suitcases quickly make a barren room a home, a personal statement about its occupants. Though it sometimes rankles parents, the term *home* is accurate. For many students, the dorm room they take over on move-in day is the first "owned" space they've ever occupied. Not quite their own, but definitely not their parents'. They greet the room as a blank canvas and spend the next nine months imprinting it with their own style and personality. It's a heady experience, typically one long remembered. But please, no nails, hammers, or screws.

Though each college has its own move-in-day traditions, all schools work hard to put their best foot forward. Flags fly, school spirit abounds, and legions of returning students greet new students and their families to help them move their gear from vehicle to residence hall. College presidents often pitch in, perhaps the only time students will see them in blue jeans and polo shirts. The atmosphere is decidedly festive, and it should be. It's the opportunity for our colleges to greet new students and their families and welcome them to our community.

And it signals the beginning of a new year, when all things are possible. Perhaps more than any other day of the academic year, including commencement, move-in day symbolizes promise and hope. No one is certain how it will all turn out, including the students themselves, but no other day of the year features the same kind of anticipatory buzz.

Everything rational that went into the college decision-making process typically vanishes on move-in day, overwhelmed by the swell of emotion. Without being overly maudlin about it, for families, move-in day marks a parting of ways of sorts. For our daughters and sons, it represents a start, the beginning of the yellow brick road to adulthood and independence. For most, it signals a moment to look forward to what could be. For parents, it's often the opposite, a conclusion—a significant change in the life that has defined family over the many prior years. While we too, as parents, delight at the promise of the future, we also see the memories of the past. Regardless of whether our daughter or son lives on campus or off campus, move-in day forces us to recall the first day of kindergarten and to wonder how the time in between passed so quickly. What happened to the cherubic child? What has happened to us, the parents? I have never experienced a move-in day where the magma of emotion did not lie just below the surface. For parents, it's a day we are allowed to feel both happy and sad at the same time.

Though I have participated in move-in days for nearly two decades as a staff member, I experienced all of those emotions as a parent when we moved in our oldest son. My professional brain and experience said, "This is great; all will be well. This is just another step forward." But my heart could not escape the feeling of change and even loss. For my son, it was move-in day. For me, it felt more like move-out day—a hard transition point from one moment in life, family, and parenthood to another. Those emotions pass. Humans are adaptable, after all. But for one brief and clear moment, the whole of a past and the future all came together. Like few other times in life, yin-yang symbolizes move-in day.

Curiously, the roles and emotions of move-in day often flip by commencement day. For students, move-in day represents a great leap forward toward independence. Even though they surely have doubts and fears about the days, months, and years to come, and they surely experience some of the same anxieties about separation from family, the shiny newness of the experience reigns. They are schooled to let go on move-in day. By commencement day, though, the reality of what lies ahead—the uncertainty of prospects and the impending certainty of adulthood and independence—often acts as a veil. I have always found college seniors to be among the most wistful people I have ever met, excited about what comes next but acutely aware that a wonderful stage of their life has passed. Parents, on the other hand, often view commencement as a kind of emancipation day. Having had several years to become accustomed to life without their son or daughter in it every day, commencement represents a rite of passage to real adulthood. And the end of tuition payments. Each a cause for great rejoicing. Parents are almost never wistful at commencement. Call it the wisdom of age for students and parents alike.

Dis-Orientation

There is perhaps no more confident creature on earth than an 18-year-old. It seems that the nadir of parental intelligence, at least according to our children, occurs when they're somewhere around age 18. "Dad, you just don't get it," or "Mom, you just don't understand" represent the terms of art—the ultimate shutdown expressions symbolizing how out of touch we are with the true complexities of reality and life in a modern world. Though those sentiments are exasperating at times, I have to admit I (sometimes) appreciate the confidence and conviction that lie behind them. Still, most young people cannot yet know that they will spend the rest of their lives navigating, sometimes successfully, other times not, the complexities of reality and all of its gray spaces.

   As they are when they leave home, so they are when they arrive at college—at least initially. National research bears this out. In the fall of 2016, nearly three-quarters of all new entering students at four-year colleges nationally rated their academic ability as above average or in the top 10 percent compared to their peers of similar age—statistically impossible, of course, but a clear expression of personal confidence.[1] Almost eight in ten described their critical thinking skills as either a major strength or at least somewhat strong. Six in ten rated their intellectual self-confidence as above average. In other words, most new undergraduate students enter college brimming with confidence and expecting to succeed, which is a terrific way to begin.

For some, and perhaps many, that sense of self-confidence may be little more than bravado acting as a security blanket. Four in ten new college students nationally report that they frequently felt overwhelmed by all they had to do during their senior year in high school. Less than half rate their social self-confidence as above average in relation to their peers. The pressure of school, the pressure of getting into college, the pressure to succeed often weigh heavily on the minds of new students as they begin their college careers.

Fit, an important but ultimately imaginary consideration before the point of choosing a college, becomes very real on move-in day and in the days and weeks that follow. "Will I find friends? Will I like my roommate, or even get along with him or her? Will I be lonely on campus? Will I fit in here?" These concerns also create anxiety in students leaving home for the first time and moving into campus residence halls.

Our daughters and sons leave the temple of the familiar for something new and exciting, but decidedly unfamiliar. As we drop them off, as parents, we worry about the very same things. Many students will struggle, some academically, some socially, others both. That clearly is difficult for us as parents. But keep in mind that college is set up to be disorienting or, at its best, re-orienting. From the first day they arrive on campus, students are thrown into a stew of newness. They meet new people and must form new social groups, sometimes for the first time in many years. Most acquire a roommate—which for some will be the first time in their lives they will share a room with someone (and have to adapt to habits unlike their own). Some have traveled long distances to college and encounter new or different cultural expectations. All will face new and significant academic expectations. All will have the freedom, and responsibility, to make their own choices, for good or ill. Colleges use noble language to describe this process: discovery, exploration, agency, responsibility, efficacy, independence. All of those words are true, but they often do not appear so neat or simple in the early days or weeks of college. College, like life, can be messy, which is what makes it both wonderful and challenging at the same time. Students are faced with both new opportunities and new challenges—and they need to develop the navigational skills to manage both.

Tempting as it is as a parent to fix a mess (a practice we become accustomed to from their birth), listening most often is the best strategy. Listen with both your head and your heart to their hopes, experiences, and concerns. As often as possible, ask guiding questions that empower them to seek their own solutions or discover their own path. We cannot live on campus with them nor can we live their lives for them. But as we have throughout their lives, we can guide, encourage, and soothe at appropriate times, managing our own worries and fears to help them become the independent, confident, and mature adults our own parents encouraged us to become. The circle of life goes on.

Think Different

College coursework is not simply a continuation of high school. It comes with significantly higher academic expectations—new material, studied more deeply, more intensively, and more quickly than anything in a typical high school. But if that were it, a successful experience would require little more than adapting to a new pace of learning. It is much more than that. For the first time in many of their academic lives, students will encounter teachers, classes, and classmates who challenge not just their understanding of issues or the world but also their values. I have vivid memories of a class in my first year of college, taught by a professor beloved by students and who would eventually become my advisor and a mentor. The professor, known by all students and faculty simply as "Murph," was an imposing guy—physically large, loud, brash, and strong willed. Early in the semester, he asked a student to read a paper she had prepared for class that day. She began with the line, "I feel . . ." I do not recall what she said next, and it likely didn't matter, because Murph immediately stood up, pounded on his table in front of the class, and bellowed, "Dammit, I don't care what you feel! I want to know what you *THINK*!" I do recall all of us more or less cowering in the aftermath, mostly thankful we weren't the recipient of his wrath. But we were. It wasn't so much that he didn't care about our feelings (he in fact cared deeply about his students), but more that he wanted us to understand why and how we got there. It was a variant of the Socratic dictum that the unexamined life is not worth living.

I have never forgotten that experience. It was in many ways symbolic of what a strong college education is or should be about. An education's primary purpose is not to tell students *what* to think but instead to teach them to learn *how* to think about important issues, how to thoughtfully weigh questions, and how to develop their own values, direction, and sense of purpose. That comes less in the form of simple affirmation and more often in the form of probing, questioning, and reflecting. The objective is not to lead students to reject all they have believed and understood up to that point in their lives, but rather to encourage them to think about, and perhaps to think differently about, their world. College is much less about working hard (though it absolutely requires that) than it is about thinking hard.

For all of those reasons, a new college student can be quite challenging for parents—especially when our sons or daughters come home and announce they no longer believe in something important to us. This can be highly difficult on moral or values-based issues. Responding to a survey, a parent of a first-year student at my college wrote that his son was "straying from his faith," questioning beliefs and practices deeply important to their family. The tone of the parent's note reflected not only anger but also a deep sense of sadness and loss. It's a common story. Many new students will confront difficult or challenging questions about their values and beliefs—political, religious, social, and moral. That's normal. Those questions will fundamentally alter the worldviews of some, leading them to new convictions and new life paths. Those questions will cause others to develop a deeper and richer understanding of views and values they may largely have assumed before. In either case, parenting a college student requires equal measures of patience, fortitude, and understanding.

The Room at the Top of the Stairs

Whether they live on campus or at home, sending a child to college signals a significant change in the routines of family life. Yesterday they were children (though they likely didn't see it that way). The rules and norms of everyday family life applied more or less simply. Today they are young adults, with newfound independence. They imagine "the places they'll go," while parents have to pivot quickly from "the places we've been." All parents must make the transition, but often not without at least some feeling of disequilibrium.

Parents often worry after they drop their children off at college. What was up to that point an abstraction—a date in some far-off future—is now suddenly real. "Will my child be safe? How will they handle choices about sex, drugs, and alcohol? Will they find good friends? Will they still think about us at home?" Hopefully we have prepared them for this moment and those choices. Though many young people confront these choices long before they arrive in college, they now will make them outside of the watchful cover of home. Parenting a college student is a trust walk. We have to trust that we have prepared them to act and choose in their own best interests, to know both their possibilities and their limits.

College demands a new adult-to-adult relationship with our children—a rite of passage for child and parent alike. We become less like managing partners and more like guides, perhaps even sages (at least occasionally). We need to listen, direct, and intervene more carefully, and often in more nuanced ways, than we did when they were younger. While sometimes difficult, this new relationship need not be a source of pain or angst. We can take great pride in watching our children become the remarkable, self-sufficient, confident adults we have always hoped they would become.

I struggled with the transition in my oldest son's first year of college, wondering how to comport myself as the parent of an adult college student. He attends the college where I work, which meant I would see him occasionally (though not nearly as often as either he or I likely imagined). He traveled only nine miles from home to campus and appropriately sought to create an experience and space that was all his own. He craved the opportunity to define an identity distinct from home and family. He did not come home until Thanksgiving of his first year and communicated with my wife and me infrequently. I wrestled throughout his first semester with how often to text or call him, and even then with what to say or ask. I didn't want to make it seem like I was prying or directing his experience. When he came home for an extended holiday break that first December, we had to sort out which home rules now applied. His bedroom remained his space, but he was now part resident, part guest. It took me a long time to give myself the freedom to redefine our relationship—a new adult-to-adult relationship. Now, late in his college experience, we talk both more frequently and more comfortably. The awkward moments that defined the early days have been replaced by more genuine conversation. I still offer advice, both when asked and independently, but I've learned to listen better—and to discern when he needs advice and when he just needs to vent. As my next children get ready to head to college, I hope I've learned valuable lessons that will prepare me for their experiences, which will be distinctly their own. I make no claim to perfection, nor do I believe that having gone through this that I have figured it all out. But like a student, I do hope that I continue to learn, both from success and from failure. I've resigned myself to the understanding that my wife and I will never discover our children's owner manual. There is only trial and error. And love. And that will certainly do.

Dear Children

I wrote the letter below to my oldest son and gave it to him on his move-in day. I hope he found it helpful, or at least vaguely interesting and something to return to later in his life. I plan to write similar letters to all of my children as they leave for college.

Dear Andrew,

I have been thinking for a while about what kind of advice to leave you as you head to college. It's easier for me to write than to say. Eighteen years have gone by in the blink of an eye. You have become an extraordinary young man. We've tried our best to be good parents (Mom is better at that than I am!). And now you are on the cusp of building your own independent life. So, as you begin college, here is my best attempt at advice. Call it "Dad's Top Ten List."

1. **Be true to yourself and to your values**. Be your own person, not what you think others want you to be. Respect yourself. Respect others. Demand and expect that they respect you.

2. **Get involved**. College is amazing. There are a million different things to do—clubs, lectures, arts. Soak it up. Spread your wings. Explore. Go to something you never thought of or thought you would like.

3. **Make good choices**. You knew that would be on this list. You will face many different choices, some easy, some difficult. Always keep the end in mind. Use item 1 as a guide.

4. **Choose your friends wisely**. Many of the people you meet in college will become your closest friends for the rest of your life.

They will be like brothers and sisters. Make sure you actually like and respect them.

5. **Surround yourself with interesting people**. They will make you both wiser and more interesting.

6. **Feed your mind, body, and spirit**. Take care of yourself. Study hard. Work out. Go to church (at least pay attention to your spirit).

7. **Stop at "buzzed."** Practical parental and life advice. Don't be the guy who wakes up hungover and can't remember the night before. It's stupid, unattractive, and unhealthy, and can be dangerous. College social culture is a lot of fun, but handle it with care. Don't abuse it and don't get caught up in it. Know when fun ends and stupid begins.

8. **Never, ever, ever mix sex and alcohol**. It can have ruinous lifetime consequences for at least two people.

9. **As for sex generally, think above the shoulders not below the waist**. It's not a game, and it shouldn't be just a casual thing. Understand consent: no always means no. And consent goes two ways: Two people have to consent, not just one. See item 1.

10. **Ask questions and speak for yourself**. Be your own best advocate. Find your voice and then use it.

Know that you always have been and always will be deeply loved. Mom and I will always be there for you. And don't forget to call home. We sometimes just need to hear your voice.

With all my love,
Dad

Acknowledgments

This book began with a simple idea—that a book written in the form of a series of letters would provide an interesting and valuable way to talk about college preparation. I had initially intended to write each chapter myself as a "Dear Parent" letter. But a casual conversation at a conference with my friend and colleague Rachelle Hernandez reshaped my thinking and the narrative. "Don't write all of the letters yourself," she said. "Ask us—your friends from around the country—to write them. We'll say yes if you ask!" And so a new book was born.

I am deeply grateful to all of my letter-writing colleagues: Pam Horne, Matt Malatesta, Karen Cooper, Renee and Rick Bischoff, Greg Walker, Kristin Tichenor, Brian Lindeman, Eric Staab, Phil Trout, Robert Piechota, Tom Nelson Laird, Rodney Morrison, Kaya Henderson, Scott Friedhoff, Jon Boeckenstedt, Jillian Hiscock, Betsy Johnson-Miller and Shane Miller, Jody Terhaar, Carol and Brian Bruess, and especially Rachelle Hernandez, who provided the core inspiration for the letter idea and to whom I owe a great debt of gratitude. I provided everyone with a different prompt question about some aspect of college preparation and asked them to write both as a parent and as an education professional. I knew that melding the head and heart would make for a challenging exercise—and nearly everyone told me it was harder to write than they thought it would be—but I was blown away by what I received. I learned a great deal from everyone and thank them for sharing their family stories and experiences, as well as their many years of professional experience and wisdom. I truly am blessed to count as friends and colleagues so many wise, interesting, and wonderful people.

I thank Greg Britton at Johns Hopkins University Press for his encouragement and guidance—and for having the confidence in me to ask for a second book. He suggested I think about writing a book aimed at parents about college admissions. As the parent of four children, with one in college already and two in high school, it seemed a natural. But as my letter writers said, getting from an interesting idea to a conversational book centered on letters proved a more challenging writing proposition than it sounded. It was difficult but worth every minute. I think Greg knew it would be a challenge, but his confidence never wavered. I hope he enjoys this book and finds it useful as his own daughter prepares for college.

I am indebted to my friend Chris Farrell. If you listen at all to National Public Radio, you likely have heard Chris's wise counsel on matters of personal finance. He is a master of translating complex financial issues into useful bits and bytes of personal information and wisdom. I owe him a dinner. Among the books Chris has written himself are two fine volumes: *The New Frugality* and *Unretirement* (both from Bloomsbury Press). I highly recommend both.

Thank you to Sara Kyle, Karen Backes, and Mary Nicklawske for reading the manuscript and assuaging my worries about the content, tone, and usefulness of the book. I appreciate your counsel and words of encouragement.

I am deeply grateful to my childhood friend, Chuck Pederson, for his wise editorial assistance. Chuck and I have known each other since we were 7 years old—now too many years to tally the total. He is among the smartest and most erudite people I know and was the only Moody Blues fan I knew when we were in high school a million years ago. Chuck edited the initial manuscript and significantly improved the flow and the narrative.

I owe a special thanks to my niece, Grace McGee, whose story I introduced early in the book. Grace is self-assured and mature beyond her young years. I admire the college choice she made and am grateful she willingly agreed to share her story. College comes in many, many forms.

Finally, and most of all, I thank my family, both for allowing me (more or less) to share stories of them and for indulging me (more or less) as I wrote the book. I made a habit of making them listen to me read paragraphs as I was writing because I wanted to know how they sounded, which more than once earned the response, "Mom, please make Dad stop!" This book in the end is both a professional reflection and a personal family reflection. I am blessed to have a loud, active, often chaotic, but always interesting and entertaining family. When I wrote my first book, my middle sons, both teenagers, asked, "Dad, is anyone *normal* going to read this book?" I have to admit, I had to think carefully about that at the time. This book is for parents. I hope they think we are normal. Andrew, Nick, Ben, and Kate: though we have never found your owner's manuals, you have provided the light of our lives. It has been the greatest of joys to watch you grow up and become remarkable young men and women. Never let go of your dreams. My wife, Ann, is the leader of our merry band. She leads with patience, love, kindness, and remarkable selflessness. We are all better for it. With all my love, this is the book of our life!

Notes

CHAPTER ONE. DISCOVER COLLEGE

Epigraph: Goodreads, Anaïs Nin Quotes. https://www.goodreads.com/author/quotes /7190.Ana_s_Nin.

1. Visit the Gallup-Purdue Index at http://www.gallup.com/topic/gallup_purdue _index.aspx for a fascinating review of the importance of a variety of college experiences on postcollege success.

2. United States Census Bureau, Current Population Survey, Table A-2, "Percent of People 25 Years and Over Who Have Completed High School or College, by Race, Hispanic Origin and Sex: Selected Years 1940 to 2017." https://www.census.gov/data/tables /time-series/demo/educational-attainment/cps-historical-time-series.html. Back in those days, counting conventions apparently did not include educational attainment of less than four years.

3. National Center for Education Statistics, *Digest of Education Statistics: 2016*, US Department of Education, Tables 302.10, "Recent High School Completers and Their Enrollment in College, by Sex and Level of Institution: 1960 through 2016"; 303.10, "Total Fall Enrollment in Degree-Granting Postsecondary Institutions, by Attendance Status, Sex of Student, and Control of Institution: Selected Years, 1947 through 2026"; and 317.10, "Degree-Granting Postsecondary Institutions, by Control and Level of Institution: Selected Years, 1949–50 through 2015–16."

4. For a fascinating and lucid account of the pace of change, read Thomas Friedman's book, *Thank You for Being Late* (New York: Farrar, Straus and Giroux, 2016).

5. Pablo Picasso: Paintings, Quotes, and Biography. http://www.pablopicasso.org /quotes.jsp.

6. National Center for Education Statistics, Classification of Instructional Programs (CIP), US Department of Education. https://nces.ed.gov/ipeds/cipcode /Default.aspx?y=55.

7. United States Census Bureau, Table A-6, "Age Distribution of College Students 14 Years Old and Over, by Sex: October 1947 to 2016." https://www.census.gov/data /tables/time-series/demo/school-enrollment/cps-historical-time-series.html.

8. National Center for Education Statistics, *Digest of Education Statistics: 2016*, Table 303.5, "Total Fall Enrollment in Degree-Granting Postsecondary Institutions, by Level of Enrollment, Control and Level of Institution, Attendance Status, and Age of Student: 2015." https://nces.ed.gov/programs/digest/d16/tables/dt16_303.50.asp ?current=yes.

9. Yogi Berra, *The Yogi Book* (New York: Workman, 1998).

10. National Center for Education Statistics, *Digest of Education Statistics: 2016*, Table 303.5.

11. Peter Thiel. "Thinking Too Highly of Higher Ed," *Washington Post* [Op-ed], November 21, 2014. https://www.washingtonpost.com/opinions/peter-thiel-thinking -too-highly-of-higher-ed/2014/11/21/f6758fba-70d4-11e4-893f-86bd390a3340_story .html?utm_term=.24aeeffd8153.

12. K. Eagan, E. B. Stolzenberg, H. B. Zimmerman, M. C. Aragon, H. Whang Sayson, and C. Rios-Aguilar, *The American Freshman: National Norms Fall 2016* (Los Angeles: Higher Education Research Institute [HERI], UCLA, 2017). https://www.heri.ucla.edu /monographs/TheAmericanFreshman2016.pdf.

13. Pew Research Center. "The Rising Cost of *Not* Going to College," February 2014. https://www.pewsocialtrends.org/2014/02/11/the-rising-cost-of-not-going-to-college/.

14. United States Census Bureau, Current Population Survey, Table PINC-04, "Educational Attainment—People 18 Years Old and Over, by Total Money Earnings, Work Experience, Age, Race, Hispanic Origin, and Sex." https://www.census.gov/data /tables/time-series/demo/income-poverty/cps-pinc/pinc-04.html.

15. B. Hershein and M. Kearney, *Major Decisions: What Graduates Earn over Their Lifetimes*, The Hamilton Project, September 2014. For a fascinating view of earnings and occupations by age and over the course of a career by college major, visit The Hamilton Project's interactive site: http://www.hamiltonproject.org/charts/median_earnings _for_largest_occupations.

16. US Bureau of Labor Statistics, *Employment Situation*, custom tabulation from Federal Reserve Economic Data, Federal Reserve Bank of St. Louis (FRED). https:// fred.stlouisfed.org/.

17. US Bureau of Labor Statistics, *Employment Situation*, Supplemental Table A-5, "Employment Situation of the Civilian Non-institutional Population by Educational Attainment, July 2017." I have only examined overall labor force participation. Participation rates by men and women, for example, are significantly different from each other.

18. A. Carnevale, N. Smith, and J. Strohl, *Recovery: Job Growth and Education Requirements through 2020* (Center for Education and the Workforce: Georgetown University, June 2013). https://cew.georgetown.edu/cew-reports/recovery-job-growth -and-education-requirements-through-2020/.

19. Pew Research Center. "The Rising Cost of *Not* Going to College."

CHAPTER TWO. SCHOOL MATTERS

Epigraph: Vince Lombardi. http://www.vincelombardi.com/quotes.html.

1. The proprietary research was conducted by Strategic Resource Partners and Hardwick Day for Minnesota's private colleges. More than 200 Minnesota parents of middle school students were randomly selected and surveyed. The survey also included parents of high school students and was designed to assess family behaviors and attitudes regarding the selection and financing of higher education.

2. J. Wallace and L. Heffernan, "Advice College Admissions Officers Give Their Own Kids," *New York Times*, March 17, 2016. https://well.blogs.nytimes.com/2016/03/17 /advice-college-admissions-officers-give-their-own-kids/.

3. Wallace and Heffernan.

CHAPTER THREE. FIT

Epigraph: Carl Sandburg, "Who Am I?" https://www.poetryfoundation.org.

1. K. Eagan et al., *The American Freshman: National Norms Fall 2016.*

2. Recall Nike's advertisement during the 1996 Atlanta Olympics, which used the phrase to convey the idea of best. The ad was widely criticized at the time for its decidedly unsportsmanlike and competitively unhealthy tone—though it surely captured our cultural fascination with finishing on top.

3. Data from *Peterson's* online college search. http://www.petersons.com/college-search.aspx.

4. Sallie Mae and Ipsos Public Affairs. *How America Pays for College 2017,* Table 31, "Attitudes toward College, Scale 1–5," July 2017. https://salliemae.newshq.businesswire.com/sites/salliemae.newshq.businesswire.com/files/doc_library/file/How_America_Pays_for_College_2017_Report.pdf.

5. K. Eagan et al., *The American Freshman: National Norms Fall 2016.*

6. E. Venit, "How Late Is Too Late? Myths and Facts about the Consequences of Switching College Majors," Education Advisory Board, Student Success Collaborative, 2016. https://www.eab.com/technology/student-success-collaborative/members/white-papers/major-switching.

CHAPTER FOUR. MONEY MATTERS

Epigraph: Ayn Rand, cited in *Forbes,* "Top 100 Money Quotes of All Time." https://www.forbes.com/sites/robertberger/2014/04/30/top-100-money-quotes-of-all-time/#ef58d064998d.

1. J. Jones, "U.S. Parents' College Funding Worries Are Top Money Concern," Gallup, April 20, 2015. http://www.gallup.com/poll/182537/parents-college-funding-worries-top-money-concern.aspx.

2. United States Census Bureau, *Current Population Survey,* Annual Social and Economic Supplements, Table F-3, 2016.

3. National Center for Education Statistics, *Digest of Education Statistics: 2017,* US Department of Education, Table 330.10, "Average Undergraduate Tuition and Fees and Room and Board Rates Charged for Full-Time Students in Degree-Granting Postsecondary Institutions, by Level and Control of Institution: 1963–64 through 2015–16." https://nces.ed.gov/programs/digest/d16/tables/dt16_330.10.asp?current=yes.

4. Sallie Mae and Ipsos Public Affairs, *How America Pays for College, 2017,* July 2017, Table 40, "Elimination of Colleges Based on Cost, Cumulative after Saying Yes at Each Point." https://salliemae.newshq.businesswire.com/sites/salliemae.newshq.businesswire.com/files/doc_library/file/How_America_Pays_for_College_2017_Report.pdf.

5. The College Board, Advocacy and Policy Center, *Trends in Student Aid, 2016,* Table 1, "Total Student Aid and Nonfederal Loans in 2016 Dollars (in Millions), 2006–07 to 2016–17," October 2016. https://trends.collegeboard.org/student-aid/figures-tables/total-student-aid-and-nonfederal-loans-2016-dollars-over-time.

6. The College Board, Advocacy and Policy Center, *Trends in Student Aid 2017,* Table 1. Author's calculations: I assumed a modest $1,500 allowance for textbook and miscellaneous costs at private and public four-year colleges and universities, and $500 at two-year colleges.

7. The College Board, *Trends in Student Aid 2016.*

8. If you are economically inclined, I recommend you read Robert Archibald and David Feldman's fine book, *Why Does College Cost So Much?* (New York: Oxford University Press, 2011). Both economists at William and Mary College, they explain in reasonably simple economic terms the difference between cost and price and the factors that influence both.

9. National Center for Education Statistics, *Digest of Education Statistics: 2017*, US Department of Education, Table 334.10, "Expenditures of Public Degree-Granting Postsecondary Institutions, by Purpose of Expenditure and Level of Institution: Selected Years, 2007–08 through 2014–15"; and 334.20, "Expenditures of Public Degree-Granting Postsecondary Institutions, by Level of Institution, Purpose of Expenditure, and State or Jurisdiction: 2011–12 through 2014–15." https://nces.ed.gov/programs/digest/current_tables.asp.

10. National Center for Education Statistics, *Digest of Education Statistics: 2017*, US Department of Education, Table 314.10. https://nces.ed.gov/programs/digest/current_tables.asp.

11. H. Bowen, *The Costs of Higher Education* (San Francisco: Jossey-Bass, 1980).

12. National Center for Education Statistics, *Digest of Education Statistics: 2017*, US Department of Education, Table 331.20. https://nces.ed.gov/programs/digest/d16/tables/dt16_331.20.asp?current=yes.

13. The College Board, *Trends in Student Aid, 2016*. Table 1A.

14. Donghoon Lee, "Household Debt and Credit: Student Debt," Federal Reserve Bank of New York, February 28, 2013. In September 2017, the Federal Reserve Bank of New York reported that outstanding student loan debt totaled $1.36 trillion.

15. The College Board, *Trends in Student Aid, 2016*.

16. "Savings at Lowest Rate since Depression," CBS News, February 1, 2007. The full online story is available at http://www.cbsnews.com/stories/2007/02/01/business/main2422489.shtml. I share this story with the gracious approval of my brother and sister-in-law.

17. Sallie Mae and Ipsos Public Affairs, *How America Saves for College, 2016*, September 2016, Table 7.

18. Sallie Mae and Ipsos Public Affairs, *How America Saves for College, 2016*, Table 10.

19. Board of Governors of the Federal Reserve System, *Report on the Well-Being of U.S. Households in 2015*, May 2016. https://www.federalreserve.gov/publications/files/2016-report-economic-well-being-us-households-201705.pdf.

20. E. Bloom, "Here's How Many Americans Have Nothing at All Saved for Retirement," CNBC, June 13, 2017. https://www.cnbc.com/2017/06/13/heres-how-many-americans-have-nothing-at-all-saved-for-retirement.html.

21. Sallie Mae and Ipsos Public Affairs, *How America Saves for College, 2016*, Table 3.

22. B. Schwartz, *The Paradox of Choice: Why More Is Less* (New York: Harper Perennial, 2004).

23. Sallie Mae and Ipsos Public Affairs, *How America Pays for College, 2017*, August 2017.

CHAPTER FIVE. CHOOSE

Epigraph: Dr. Seuss, *Oh, The Places You'll Go!* (New York: Random House, 1990).

1. "Top 100—Lowest Acceptance Rates," *U.S. News and World Report.* https://www
.usnews.com/best-colleges/rankings/lowest-acceptance-rate.

2. National Center for Education Statistics, Integrated Postsecondary Education
Data System (IPEDS) Data Center. Author's calculations. https://nces.ed.gov/ipeds
/Home/UseTheData.

3. National Center for Education Statistics, *Digest of Education Statistics: 2016*,
Table 305.40, "Acceptance Rates; Number of Applications, Admissions, and Enrollees;
and Enrollees' SAT and ACT Scores for Degree-Granting Postsecondary Institutions
with First-Year Undergraduates, by Control and Level of Institution: 2015–16." https://
nces.ed.gov/programs/digest/d16/tables/dt16_305.40.asp.

4. G. Rosenblum, "How to Turn College Rejection into a Lucky Break," *Minneapolis
Star Tribune,* April 17, 2017. http://www.startribune.com/rosenblum-how-to-turn-college
-rejection-into-a-lucky-break/419429794/.

5. National Center for Education Statistics, *Digest of Education Statistics: 2016*,
US Department of Education, Table 302.10. https://nces.ed.gov/programs/digest/d16
/tables/dt16_302.10.asp?current=yes.

6. K. Eagan et al., *The American Freshman: National Norms Fall 2016.*

7. Peace Bransberger and Demarée K. Michelau. *Knocking at the College Door:
Projections of High School Graduates,* 9th ed. (Boulder, CO: Western Interstate Com-
mission for Higher Education, 2016).

8. S. Jaschik and D. Lederman, "The 2016 Survey of College & University Admissions Directors," *Inside Higher Ed* and Gallup, September 2016.

9. K. Eagan, E. B. Stolzenberg, A. K. Bates, M. C. Aragon, M. R. Suchard, and
C. Rios-Aguilar, *The American Freshman: National Norms for Fall 2015* (Los Angeles:
Higher Education Research Institute [HERI], UCLA, 2016). https://www.heri.ucla.edu
/monographs/TheAmericanFreshman2015.pdf.

10. M. Clinedinst, A.-M. Koranteng, and T. Nicola, *2015 State of College Admission*,
National Association for College Admission Counseling, 2015. https://www.nacacnet
.org/globalassets/documents/publications/research/2015soca.pdf.

11. National Association for College Admission Counseling, *Statement of Principles
of Good Practice and Other Policies.* https://www.nacacnet.org/advocacy—ethics
/statement-of-principles-of-good-practice/.

CHAPTER SIX. A NEW CHAPTER

Epigraph: The Thomas Merton Center at Bellarmine University. http://merton.org
/Roots/.

1. K. Eagan et al., *The American Freshman: National Norms Fall 2016.*

Index